CRASH PROOF WEALTH

The Roadmap to Wealth and Independence
with Peace of Mind

BRETT KITCHEN & TROY RAGAN

CRASH PROOF WEALTH

The Roadmap to Wealth and Independence with Peace of Mind

ISBN 987-1-7351491-3-4 paperback

Printed in the United States of America

Year of First Printing: 2021

Cover Design by: Ken Wilcox

Disclaimer

While great efforts have been taken to provide accurate and current information regarding the covered material, neither Crash Proof Wealth nor Brett Kitchen or Troy Ragan are responsible for any errors or omissions or for the results obtained from the use of this information.

The name 'Crash Proof Wealth' is a marketing concept and does not guarantee or imply that you will become wealthy. The act of purchasing any book, course, or financial product holds no such guarantees.

The ideas, suggestions, general principles, and conclusions presented here are subject to local, state, and federal laws and regulations and revisions of same and are intended for informational purposes only. All information in this report is provided "as is," with no guarantee of completeness, accuracy, or timeliness regarding the results obtained from the use of this information. And without warranty of any kind, express or implied, including, but not limited to warranties of performance, merchantability, and fitness for a particular purpose. Your use of this information is at your own risk.

You assume full responsibility and risk of loss resulting from the use of this information. Brett Kitchen and/or Troy Ragan and Crash Proof Wealth will not be liable for any direct, special, indirect, incidental, consequential, or punitive damages or any other damages whatsoever, whether in an action based upon a statute, contract, tort (including, but not limited to negligence), or otherwise, relating to the use of this information.

In no event will Brett Kitchen and/or Troy Ragan, Crash Proof Wealth, or their related partnerships or corporations, or the partners, agents, or employees of Brett Kitchen and/or Troy Ragan or Crash Proof Wealth be liable to you or anyone else for any decision made or action taken in reliance on the information in this book or for any consequential, special, or similar damages, even if advised of the possibility of such damages.

Neither Brett Kitchen, Troy Ragan, nor Crash Proof Wealth is engaged in rendering legal, accounting, or other professional services. Therefore if accounting, financial, legal, or tax advice is required, the services of a competent professional should be sought.

Facts and information in this book are believed to be accurate at the time of publication and may become outdated by marketplace changes or conditions, new or revised laws, or other circumstances. All figures and examples in this report are based on rates and assumptions no later than May 2017. Rates and assumptions are not guaranteed and may be subject to change. As in all assumptions and examples, individual results may vary based on a wide range of factors unique to each person's situation. All data provided in this book are to be used for informational purposes only. Any slights against individuals, companies, or organizations are unintentional.

For my wife, Carson. You constantly amaze me with all that you do, and you inspire me to be the best me I can be. And for my five kiddos. I can't believe you've all grown up now, but I'm so proud of the young adults you're becoming. You all challenge me in your own ways, and I believe I am a better man for it.
I love you guys!

TROY RAGAN

For my wife, Tiffani, who puts up with endless hours of work and the roller coaster of life married to an entrepreneur, my kiddos, who love it when dad gets home, and my parents, Dan and Becky Kitchen, who taught me the value of hard work, integrity, and good living.
I love you all very much.

BRETT KITCHEN

CONTENTS

FOR SKEPTICS ONLY

What does Crash Proof Wealth mean? Here's what it isn't: stuffing your money in a mattress or hunkering down with gold bullion. You don't even need a million bucks to be in the club. *Becoming wealthy beyond Wall Street* means you've started on a path that could keep your money safely growing over time. Rest assured, for the average American, the dream of becoming a millionaire is not out of reach. In fact, the blueprint is sitting in your hands right now. Here are some of the most common questions people have had before joining the ranks of the wealthy beyond Wall Street.

1. Is it really possible to become wealthy outside of Wall Street?

Actually, it depends. It's not for everyone. Some people are addicted to the ups and downs of the market—and believe it or not, they can't understand how their money can safely grow each and every day regardless of the economy, market, or latest bad news on TV. If that's you, then sorry, now is the time to shut the cover on this book and pass it on to someone who wants some diversity, a need for life insurance to manage risk, and gain peace of mind in their financial future.

2. Is it too late for me?

No way! No matter what your age, many of the concepts embraced by Americans getting wealthy outside of Wall Street can be used to grow and safeguard your money for you or your family at any time.

3. Do I have to scrimp and save and basically eat beans and rice in order to grow my money?

Nope. No dietary changes are required to join the club. In fact, once you discover how to Finance Yourself To Wealth™, you may just end up living better while saving money doing it. There's nothing like living the high life without the heavy dose of guilt or the pressure of a too-tight budget.

4. Is this just more pop culture investment advice?

This book is for anyone who would like to learn how to diversify a portion of their money outside Wall Street. The principles taught in this book have been around for years. And case studies range from start-up business owners to the average American household and anywhere in between.

5. Is this just another financial dead end? How do I know whom to trust?

Fortunately for all of us, some of the ideas we share with you in this book have been around for over 100 years. In fact, there's a good chance your parents or even grandparents used some of these lost strategies decades ago...you might say we're bringing some financial wisdom back from the dead!

6. Do I need to be a financial whiz?

Not at all. In fact, I think you'll find the whole process refreshingly simple. No monitoring of the markets and no complex calculations you need to worry about. Once you get going, becoming wealthy beyond Wall Street could happen with a dedicated long-term approach.

Section 1

STATUS QUO KILLERS

"Status quo, you know, that is Latin for 'the mess we're in.'"
— RONALD REAGAN

"Bureaucracy defends the status quo long past the time when the quo has lost its status."
—DR. LAURENCE J. PETER

Chapter 1

GROWING NEST EGGS, CHASING RETURNS, OR CASHING CHECKS?

In 2002, I was living in Colorado Springs. A pastor friend suggested I meet with someone he had been working with to earn some supplemental income (his small church couldn't afford to pay him much). I met with this gentleman and learned he was teaching seminars about risk-free investing—realizing some of the stock market's growth without the risk of market losses. I'd had a license to sell financial products since I was 19 and had made a few sales over the years. Still, I hadn't pursued an actual career in financial product sales. I attended one of his seminars and liked what I saw. I had maintained my license, so he took me on. I was looking forward to teaching my own seminars, but I would have to raise the money to cover the expenses of such an event myself.

Dinner seminars are expensive. I knew I would have to pay for the meals of all those who attended, but the most expensive part was the mass mailing costs necessary to invite folks to the event. After about six months, I could finally afford to pay for that first seminar. Thousands of invitations had been mailed, and over thirty people had RSVP'd. I was so excited.

It was mid-February 2003, and on the night of my seminar, it snowed. Big time! The Colorado sky dumped about four feet of the white stuff within a couple of hours, and no one showed up. I had just barely been able to scrape up the money to do this thing, and it had taken me six months to do so! I was devastated.

Fortunately, the gentleman who mentored me was kind enough to pay for the next seminar because of what happened. He had been training me during those initial six months. Apparently, he saw some potential and thought I'd be successful.

A month later, I taught my first seminar to a crowd of about thirty people. My new career teaching investors how to safely grow their money was officially launched.

I've got some stage experience in theater, so I really enjoyed getting up in front of people. I liked to have a lot of fun with the attendees, and I was determined to actually teach them some financial principles instead of just trying to sell them something— which proved to be a refreshingly different approach than what they were used to experiencing in other seminars.

I really miss doing the seminars. They're not really cost-effective these days because so many people are doing them, pushing hard for sales, and turning people off. But, I really had a good time with them and quickly became very successful. I truly cared about the people I was teaching. To me, they weren't just customers or prospective customers, and I think people could sense that. I really enjoyed getting to know them—learning their fears and concerns and then not just selling something, but instead creating solutions for them.

That was a long time ago.

And, while my life has taken some drastic, unplanned turns, I did discover my true career passion: financial teaching and counseling.

Only a couple years into my new career, I lost my wife to cancer. She was very young and had a brain tumor—an oligodendroglioma. We fought that sucker for six years and had a six-year-old daughter when she died (we discovered the brain tumor precisely three weeks after our daughter was born). I found myself on the business end of over a hundred thousand dollars of medical bills, and twenty years ago, that was a lot of money for me.

I wasn't in the right place mentally or emotionally to continue teaching seminars, and my funds depleted to a point where I couldn't afford to pay for them, anyway. So, I moved from Colorado to North Carolina to be closer to family. My mom had been diagnosed with breast cancer, and I wanted my daughter to have a chance to have a relationship with her grandmother.

While in North Carolina, I owned and operated a tile sales and installation business. I had once owned a high-end interior design showroom in Colorado that sold furniture, home décor, wallpaper, carpet, and lots of tile—floor tile, wall tile, shower tile, and more. New home construction was booming in Colorado, and we had a heck of a time keeping tile installers on the job. So, I learned how to install it myself, and I got pretty darn good at it.

In North Carolina, I focused on tile sales and installation—I had no desire to open a showroom and deal with the headaches of employees and overhead. I had wholesale contracts with tile showrooms for tile sales, and I hired a couple of installers to help me out with the installations. I did that for six years.

And then something happened that would change my life forever: I met an amazing woman on eHarmony.

Ironically, I had logged into my eHarmony account to reduce the geographical radius in which I allowed matches to be made—I lived in North Carolina, but I kept getting matched with women from Virginia, Tennessee, South Carolina, and Georgia.

Before I clicked on the settings tab to reduce my radius, I saw a new match with the woman I would fall in love with and eventually marry. And she lived in Georgia, *waaay* outside my preferred radius—I had no plans to move to Georgia. But she was beautiful, and her profile looked like a perfect match for me, so I sent her my "Three Questions," eHarmony's first step in reaching out to a new match.

At the same time, she had logged on to eHarmony to close her account. She was a single mom of four kids aged eight to seventeen, had just finished grad school and didn't have time for dating. Before she closed the account, though, she saw my Three Questions. She replied to my questions and sent me her Three

Questions, and two years later, I was married to my sweet wife, Carson, and living in Georgia.

Our song is *God Blessed the Broken Road* by Rascal Flatts. While expressing my vows to her at our wedding, I shared with her that I often wished to go back and make different life choices. I could have avoided some severe pain and struggles. But then I realized that if I had made just one choice differently, I may have never met her or had the chance to experience the incredible life we share together.

She had some truly painful experiences, herself, that she would have liked to have avoided, but then she may have never met me. God truly blessed our broken roads.

As I began my new life in Georgia, I started working for my new brother-in-law selling life insurance. His company taught federal employees how their benefits worked during employment and retirement. Unfortunately, feds have life insurance that gets very expensive as they approach retirement. My job was to show them less costly alternatives and sell them new policies. That was okay, and I was very successful, but I really missed teaching and counseling.

Eventually, I was promoted to the teaching position. I was amazed how many federal employees had no idea how their benefits worked. Some didn't even know they would get a pension when they retired! But after a thirty-minute Benefits Review, they found themselves thoroughly educated and extremely thankful.

Soon after, I was promoted to the counseling position. My new job was to counsel feds on how to best accomplish their goals for their TSP accounts. TSP stands for Thrift Savings Plan, which is the government's version of the 401(k). Most planned to use their TSP accounts to supplement their incomes in retirement. I soon became extremely proficient in creating the maximum income possible for them, utilizing various strategies. I was finally again fulfilling my career passion of teaching and counseling. Did I mention something about God blessing the broken road?

A couple years later, my brother-in-law sold his interest in the company to an investment firm. The new owners maintained the same business plan, so it was pretty much business as usual as I continued to hone my skills at generating income. Three years later, my brother-in-law's non-compete expired, and he asked me to partner with him in a new venture. We developed a fresh approach to counseling federal employees and created the National Employee Benefits Center.

Since then, I've shown thousands of federal employees how to use their life's savings to generate income guaranteed to continue for the rest of their lives and, if desired, continue for their spouses for the rest of their lives. It has been immensely fulfilling. I love being the good guy. Most people I counsel are terrified of the market. Sadly, the consistent advice they received was to leave their funds exposed to market risks to ensure that they'll have enough to live on in retirement.

Throughout their careers, most have experienced significant losses during market crashes. It was disappointing, but they were younger and far from retiring and had plenty of time to continue contributing to their accounts and recoup the losses. But as they got closer to retirement, they found themselves extremely nervous about potential losses. They would soon depend on these funds to assist them with their retirement expenses, and a significant loss to those funds would be devastating.

Before me, no one had shown them how to invest their money safely and still earn impressive returns while finishing their federal careers and then converting those funds into lifetime income. As I mentioned, I've shown thousands how to achieve peace of mind by converting their nest eggs to a guaranteed lifetime income

I counsel by phone and screen-share to feds all across the country, and I can't tell you how many times I could actually hear tears of relief coming from the other end of the line. I could hear the fear and stress just melt from them as I showed them how they'll never have to worry about outliving their funds. I've found myself getting a little choked up, myself, as, through those tears, they thanked me for helping them find the peace of mind they didn't know they could have. Ahh, I love what I do. I love being the good guy.

Spreadin' the Love

So, yes, I love counseling the feds. But I realized that I could teach the same strategies to regular ol' folks who aren't employed by the government. Everyone wants to be able to enjoy retirement—not just feds. No one has ever told me they hope they run out of money and have to depend on their families to take care of them. And since you're reading this book and, therefore, have an IQ over 65, I assume that you also want to enjoy retirement and maintain a decent lifestyle. I can help you with that.

Unfortunately, most financial advisors will only have a hundred or so clients during their entire careers. Of course, that's okay, but it doesn't offer extensive "training" in discovering income-producing strategies. I, on the other hand, as I find myself so fond of repeating, have had thousands of chances to "practice" honing my skills. I continue to get "practice" every day as I continue to counsel feds at NEBC. And that extensive experience and continued practice can be very beneficial to you.

What Makes a Retirement Good?

The exact answer is different for everyone, of course, but in my experience, retirement is defined by **Lifestyle**. Enjoying one's lifestyle throughout retirement equals good retirement. Conversely, not enjoying one's retirement lifestyle equals not so good retirement. So, what determines whether someone will be able to enjoy their retirement lifestyle? The ability to *purchase* that desired lifestyle.

Lifestyle is different than a standard of living. Essentially, your pre-retirement standard of living is the ability to live your life on your terms within the financial resources available to you — to have the choice to allocate earned income to pay the bills, provide for those you care about, and save for future income in retirement. After the bills are paid, YOU determine how much goes into your 401(k) or IRA, how much goes into a savings account, how much you want to save/pay for your kids' college, and so forth.

What's left of your income is what is used to purchase your Lifestyle: how often you take vacations and how much they cost, how often you go out to dinner, how often you go to the movies, theatre, etc. It's basically living your life on what you have left.

Retiring often shifts a standard of living from saving for the future to paying for the present. Hopefully, the mortgage is paid down, and the kids have finished college. After an entire nine-to-five career, lifestyle becomes the priority: paying for hobbies, cruises, buying that RV to travel the country, visiting grandkids, donating time and money to charities, etc. Of course, the bills still need to be paid, but a good retirement focuses on lifestyle.

There's a Big Difference Between Wealth and Income

Nobel Prize-Winning Economist Robert C Merton, Ph.D., was quoted as saying, **"Successful retirement is defined as a stream of income sufficient to sustain your chosen standard [of] living,** *that standard [of] living is measured by income,* **not the value of a pile of money."**[1]

Throughout our careers, the goals of saving for retirement are pretty straightforward: save as much as you can and get the best returns you can get within the limits of your risk tolerance. Then, grow, grow, grow that nest egg. Of course, results may vary, but the concept is pretty simple. It's that transition into retirement, though, that can often reduce fierce, warrior investors to timid, scaredy-cat savers.

As a matter of fact, retirees often find themselves *paralyzed* when trying to figure out how to best utilize that nest egg they worked so hard to create. In most cases, keeping their money completely safe won't earn the returns they need to afford the retirement they want, so they think they have to keep their money invested in the market.

Wall Street agrees. Unfortunately, Wall Street's message is that in order to earn the returns the investor needs to sustain their retirement lifestyle, they have to subject themselves to more risk than they're comfortable with. So not only are retirees worried about drawing down their retirement accounts too quickly, but they're also concerned (and rightfully so) about the market taking away chunks of cash from their portfolios.

Those who adhere to this traditional way of thinking— focusing on maintaining a nest egg from which to draw down in retirement—often find themselves tightening up their belts after they retire. They are afraid of having too much life at the end of their money, so they find themselves settling for a reduced lifestyle. They don't see the grandkids who live in other states as often as they want. They don't take as many trips or cruises as they had planned to take once the nine-to-five workday was behind them. And purchasing the RV is out of the question.

On the other hand, the opposite may be true. Folks retire with a nice nest egg because the market has been extremely kind to them, and they've been lulled into a false sense of security that the market will continue to provide those pre-retirement returns indefinitely. As a result, they may actually spend *more* money in retirement than when working. To them, every day is Saturday! They've worked hard all their lives, and it's time to live it up! So, they buy that RV and start checking off items on their bucket list.

They may not realize that they're depleting their nest egg much faster than they should until it's too late, and they could find themselves having to settle for a diminished lifestyle later in life. And in the midst of their over-spending, they may not only suffer a reduction in future lifestyle, but they may actually eventually run out of money if the market takes a substantial chunk of their savings away.

What about you? Do you believe focusing on growing a pile of money provides the best possibility to maintain the desired lifestyle in retirement? Of course, I realize that's the message that's been thrust upon all of us throughout our lifetimes. Still, I hope that now you're at least considering the possibility that there may be a better way to achieve the lifestyle you want in retirement.

So, I challenge you to forget fund values; **income is all that matters.** Knowing I have a million dollars doesn't tell me what kind of a life I can enjoy from that million. **What we care about is the lifestyle.** Just knowing how much money you have doesn't tell you how you can live. You need to know *how much you can* *buy.* The primary concern of the saver remains what it always has been: **Will I have sufficient income in retirement to live comfortably?**"[2]

Do you know if you'll have enough retirement income? What if you don't? Are you prepared to live on 30% or 40% of your current working income? Most people don't want that, and in many cases, it would be impossible for them to even pay the bills. It certainly would be impossible to maintain their lifestyle (unless their current lifestyle only costs them 30% or 40% of their working income, of course).

If you could convert your nest egg into an income that was guaranteed for life and not subject to market losses, would you opt for that? Just imagine never running out of money—enjoying your lifestyle for the rest of your life, no matter how long you live. Sounds good, right? Just don't tell your financial advisor about it. They'll do everything they can to convince you to leave your money in the market (and under their care earning them fees).

Believe me. I know this to be true.

I provide priority-based counseling. I first determine someone's financial priorities for the various buckets of money they have. For funds earmarked for retirement, the priority is almost always income. That's especially true for the feds. Their TSP priority is almost exclusively income. In addition to a guarantee of lifetime income, the sub-priorities are almost always the same: making sure the income would continue to the surviving spouse, getting some market growth with reduced risk, getting guaranteed growth to ensure larger income payments, making sure whatever funds are left will pass to those they care about, and keeping the fees low.

I also ask them to rate the financial concepts of liquidity, safety, and growth in the order of their importance.

Almost always, the order is safety, growth, and then liquidity. They want to keep their money safe, but not to the extent of stashing all their cash under their mattress—they also want some growth. But the kind of growth they're looking for is a "safe growth" concept. And then they want enough liquidity to provide income and be available for expenses, if necessary. They're not planning to take large withdrawals from those funds.

After I've confirmed and re-confirmed and re-re-confirmed that these are their priorities and sub-priorities, I create an income plan for them. I then show them how to get guaranteed growth with no risk while they finish their careers, how to convert that guaranteed growth to an income that's guaranteed for the rest of their life (even if they run out of money while they're living), how to ensure that the same income would continue to a surviving spouse (if applicable and desired), and how to ensure that whatever funds are left upon their death(s) is immediately available to those they care about while bypassing probate.

In many cases, depending on how much they've saved, I show them how they will be guaranteed to get a raise (sometimes a substantial raise) when they retire.

In a nutshell, I create the perfect plan for them—accomplishing EXACTLY everything that THEY wanted to achieve with their funds. But sometimes, before I can assist them in implementing the plan, they will tell me that they need to run it by their financial advisor first. And my heart breaks for them. Financial advisors would love to get those TSP funds under their care and charge management fees.

So, the follow-up appointment after the meeting with the advisor is almost always the same. I hear variations of, "I think we're going to hold off for now." "Our advisor thinks she can get us better returns." "Our advisor says your plan may miss some of the best market growth and limits our liquidity options." "Our advisor thinks we can do better."

I ask the same question every time: "So when your advisor showed you how much lifetime income they could guarantee you with no risk, how did it compare to the income I showed you?" And I usually get the same answer: "Well, he didn't show us that. But he thinks he can do better for us."

I'm just amazed at how a single conversation with a financial "advisor" can somehow magically cause someone to completely forget their priorities and revert back to the brainwashing of grow, grow, grow that nest egg. They blindly trade guaranteed lifetime income and safe returns for risky investments with no income guarantees and a lifetime of watching the market, just praying that it won't crash and burn. All for the hope of this mythical concept of "He thinks we can do better."

So, they let themselves be convinced to continue the search for income on Wall Street. A stock mutual fund portfolio certainly has the potential for growth, certainly has the potential for losses, but certainly has no guarantee to provide income. Bonds can provide income, but the ones that provide the best incomes are either risky, callable, or both.

Callable means the issuer of the bond that's paying you a nice income payment can stop the payments and pay you back the money you paid for the bond. This usually happens when interest rates have declined. The bond issuer can now offer new bonds and pay lower income payments than they're paying you. That means that if you still want bond income, you can use the same money to purchase another bond, but it will be one that pays a lower income. So not even bond income is guaranteed.

Never forget: Wall Street doesn't guarantee income. Wall Street doesn't guarantee anything except risk.

Brokers and advisors don't like to even bring up income because, in many cases, they don't have access to the products that provide income guarantees. And if they do have access to them, they often won't offer them to you because they can't charge you fees to manage them.

If brokers and advisors actually do talk about income, their discussion is likely "dumbed down" to the 4% Rule. You may have heard of this. This is the old rule-of-thumb that if one withdraws 4% of the value of their retirement accounts each year, their retirement funds will last their lifetime (assuming a normal life expectancy). Is that rule something that should be followed today?

Wade Pfau, Ph.D., professor of retirement income at The American College of Financial Services and Director of Retirement Research at McLean Asset Management, said in a Morningstar article, "The probability that the 4% rule would work is a lot lower now. It worked in the U.S. historically, but previous years never dealt with low-interest rates and high stock market valuations at the same time. So, I did some updates, and for an investor taking a moderate amount of risk, 2.4% is my equivalent of the 4% rule."[3]

How do *you* feel about only getting 2.4% each year? Can you live on that? Heck, could you even live comfortably on 4%?

Well, it depends on what you've got. If I'm counseling someone with a million dollars and they're getting their pension and Social Security, that $40,000 a year will push their retirement income up to what they're making now. Sure. But for those who have $250,000, that $10,000 a year might not really help them that much.

So, if 4% will probably not be sufficient, and if the 4% Rule is actually really around *2.4%* (according to the above Morningstar quote), what then? To find the answer to that question, you have to start training your noggin to think *outside* of Wall Street.

And you have to *want* to know the answer. Maybe you don't need income from your savings in retirement. Perhaps your pension and social security will easily pay for your desired lifestyle for the rest of your life.

If that's *not* you (it's certainly not me), ask yourself these questions: Is it important to you to maintain the lifestyle you desire throughout retirement? Is it important to you to have income that never stops? Is it important to you that the income would continue to your spouse? If these things are important to you, then, yes, you want to know the answer.

So, again, to find the answer, you have to think outside of Wall Street. Therefore, you may have to step out from the umbrella of your broker or advisor and find other tools that can actually offer you some growth with safety and income guarantees. I know it's hard to imagine moving away from the traditional growth-with-risk investment model, but in retirement, it's time to preserve your wealth, not put it at risk.

Transitioning from Accumulation to Decumulation

For most, there are three stages of investing: Accumulation, Preservation, and Decumulation (also called Distribution). The Accumulation Stage begins when we're younger and starting to save and invest for retirement and lasts until a few years before retirement. We're okay with higher risk because we won't be using that money for many years, and if we suffer some losses, there is plenty of time to recoup. The Preservation Stage is when we're getting closer to retirement. It's time to stop exposing ourselves to as much risk and focus more on preserving what we've accumulated. Finally, at some point in retirement, we enter the Decumulation Stage. It's time to use the accumulation to purchase our retirement lifestyle.

There is a lot of pressure on a nest egg during the Decumulation Stage, especially if a guarantee of income has not been established. Regular withdrawals from the portfolio to purchase a lifestyle cause a constant and consistent reduction of the funds. The potential for market losses provides even more pressure. Of course, if there is a risk of losses, there must be potential for gain, which, if realized, could ease the stress of the portfolio. However, according to Craig Israelsen, Ph.D.'s "The Surprising Math of Loss and Gain," it takes a lot more growth to recoup from a loss than just the loss itself.

For example, let's say you have a retirement account worth $100,000, and the market suffers a 50% loss. That leaves you with $50,000 and a bad case of heartburn. But thankfully, the market soon enjoys an increase of 50%. Did you earn all of your money back? No. A 50% increase of the $50,000 you had left after the loss is a gain of $25,000, providing you a new balance of only $75,000. To get back to your original $100k, the market would have to push an increase of 100% to recoup your 50% loss.

So, if traditional Wall Street investments aren't appropriate for decumulation (income), what kind of account would be best to accommodate it?

Well, let's let you decide. Pretend you were walking on the beach and found an old bottle half-buried in the sand. You popped the cork and found yourself face-to-face with the almighty Income Genie. If he said you had one wish (within reason) to create an account that would best facilitate decumulation, what would you wish for? Decent growth during market increases but safety against losses when the market went down? A guaranteed lifetime income that would continue for a surviving spouse, even if the account balance went to zero during either of your lifetimes? Continuing to get safe growth with market increases and locking in that growth each year, even while receiving income? All remaining funds being immediately available to loved ones upon your death(s)? Withdrawals any time you want? Low fees?

Of course, there is no Income Genie, so let's be realistic. There is no such account, right? Just wishful thinking—a pie in the sky fiction? Hmm...

Successfully transitioning from Accumulation to Preservation and Decumulation is critical. Sadly, in my experience, most brokers and advisors do not see much difference between the three stages. Sure, they may suggest less risky investments for older investors, but there is rarely any emphasis on decumulation and the pressures a nest egg faces during that stage.

The Greatest Risk in Retirement

There are all kinds of risks in retirement: taxes, market crashes, low-interest rates, and inflation, to name a few. There are also non-financial risks that could have a financial impact on your retirement: declining health, cognitive decline, death of a spouse, and more.

But according to those I've counseled, the biggest fear by far is running out of money before running out of life—having to depend on their family to take care of them financially later in life. The fear of such a risk is well-founded, as it describes the most significant risk in retirement: Longevity.

Some people, however, aren't as concerned about longevity, as they feel they won't live long enough in retirement to worry about running out of money. Is that an erroneous assumption?

Well, it depends on their health, of course. But, according to Wade Pfau, for a married couple 65 years old, **the most likely scenario is that one surviving member will live to age 96.**[4]

Source: calculations using Society of Actuaries Mortality Tables

---

Have you thought about living until 96? Maybe you should. Then think about your money and if you will potentially outlive it.

As few as thirty years ago, a person died after being retired an average of only 10 years. Today a retiree lives an average of over 20 years in retirement. With advances in medicine, it is predicted that the number will soon stretch into an average of 25-plus years in retirement. So, how long should your retirement savings last?

If Dr. Pfau is right, you should plan on living 30 years in retirement! On the one hand, that sounds great! But on the other, will you be able to afford to live that long and still enjoy a lifestyle?

Interestingly enough, the risk of longevity is a bit of a paradox. Most of us want to live as long as we can, and modern medicine appears to be making a longer life possible. But prescription medications and the practice of medicine are becoming exponentially more expensive. So, ironically, we'll deplete more and more of our savings to pay to live longer, which could mean a longer life with fewer savings to provide for it.

There is a genuine risk of outliving our savings (longevity). Sadly, for most, once the funds dry up, that's it. In the future, most people won't have pensions, so they will have to rely solely on social security if they exhaust their retirement savings. And for many, that won't be enough.

The Retirement Answer

So many that I've counseled were terrified of retiring. Even though they would get a federal pension and social security, that wouldn't be enough to maintain the lifestyle they wanted in retirement (federal pensions aren't as large as you might think), so they feared they had to choose between reducing their retirement lifestyle or possibly running out of money and having to depend on others. For those able to save a nest egg AND were willing to change their mindsets away from Wall Street and their financial advisors, I was able to completely alleviate those fears by providing the Retirement Answer:

The Retirement Answer, of course, is **Income**. Income guaranteed for life. Income that will never stop. Income that will continue for a surviving spouse. Income to purchase your desired lifestyle. Income, income, income...

Just knowing your income will never stop provides a great deal of certainty. "Certainty provides confidence," says Michael Finke, Ph.D. "This is one of the reasons that retirees who've incorporated guaranteed income into their retirement planning **report higher levels of satisfaction.**"[5]

You've worked hard all your life. Worrying about whether you'll have enough money and staying up nights filled with anxiety is no way to live. Your health can suffer, and that will increase your medical expenses and add even more stress.

A roadmap exists to navigate a successful retirement. If you want to get that map and discover how you can build your wealth and protect it for generations, then you're reading the right book. In the following chapters, you'll discover marvelous strategies to help you achieve the retirement you've longed for. So, if you're ready to shift your mindset from chasing returns in retirement to cashing checks to purchase the lifestyle you want, let's move on!

Chapter 2

THE INVISIBLE TAX

"Inflation is when you pay fifteen dollars for the ten-dollar haircut you used to get for five dollars when you had hair."
—SAM EWING

"Inflation is taxation without legislation"
—MILTON FRIEDMAN

"By a continuing process of inflation, government can confiscate, secretly and unobserved, an important part of the wealth of their citizens."
—JOHN MAYNARD KEYNES

Through our adventures and meeting with millionaire mentors who shared their secrets with us, it became clear that there are four major killers to creating financial independence. We call them the 4 Enemies of Wealth.

These enemies are Taxes, Market Loss, Interest, and Inflation.

We'll deal with each of them in greater detail throughout the rest of this book.

You'll discover why they are "enemies" and what you can do to overcome each of them.

The first one we'll deal with is inflation. Inflation is often misunderstood and often ignored because it's a silent killer of wealth.

You don't write a check to inflation as you do to the IRS, and you don't see money disappear from your retirement account as you do in market crashes.

So, let's look at how inflation happens. Inflation is caused by the government printing money.

A simple way to understand inflation is with an analogy.

Let's say you ask your son Johnny to make Kool-Aid for dinner. He mixes it up just right, and it tastes great. But he's *really* thirsty.

So he takes a first drink, and a second, and a few more after that. Now Johnny is in trouble. The Kool-Aid is half gone, and he knows he was supposed to save it for dinner . . . but there's no more Kool-Aid mix.

He gets a brilliant idea to fix his problem.

Instead of making more Kool-Aid, he just pours some extra water into the pitcher to fill it back up.

Obviously, that's not going to taste good, but he doesn't care because he already had his fill.

The Kool-Aid, in fact, tastes terrible. It's been diluted, so the flavor is less potent.

This is essentially what happens when the government prints money. The government is the only entity that can legally print money, and by default, gets to spend it first.

Just like Johnny got to drink the Kool-Aid while it tasted good, the government gets to spend a dollar at its full potency before it's diluted.

After Washington prints more dollars, which then circulate into the money supply, what do you think that does to the value of your money?

It becomes diluted, just like Johnny's Kool-Aid.

Once it's pushed into the economy, every other dollar in the system becomes less valuable. Your money—and my money—is worth less today than it was yesterday because of the money printing going on in Washington.

However, unlike Johnny, who only took a few drinks, the government's thirst for spending seems *unquenchable.* Therefore, they continue printing money to the point where our dollar is worth $0.43 compared to 30 years ago.[11]

This is the damage inflation does.

Take a look at this image and see if you remember paying $.99 for a gallon of gas or $5.00 to go to the movies. Of course, you do. It's not that gas is so much more expensive, or bread is so much harder to make—it's that our money is worth less now than it was 20 or 30 years ago.

MOVIE TICKET

1952	1983	2021
$.50	$3.50	$5.13

LOAF WHITE WONDER BREAD

1952	1983	2021
$.16	$.51	$2.69

AVERAGE GALLON OF GAS

1952	1983	2021
$.20	$1.24	$3.58

SNICKERS CANDY BAR

1952	1983	2021
$.05	$.40	$1.09

McDONALDS BIG MAC

1952	1983	2021
$.15	$.50	$3.99

http://www.kqbamseers.com/how-much-did-a-big-mac-cost-in-1983/5022573

This is bad in many ways. First, cost of living increases, as the price of everyday goods, rise faster than wages.

For low- to middle-income Americans living on a fixed income, inflation actually pushes people down to a lower standard of living. But it really gets ugly when you look at this in terms of retirement.

Here's why . . .

Let's assume that inflation is at 4% percent. That's a hair higher than what the government typically tells us. But it's hard to know the true inflation rate since the government has changed the way it's calculated multiple times.

(If you calculate inflation with the same measurements the government was using in the 1970s, the inflation rate for the past few years is closer to 5-10%!)[12]

We'll use the Rule of 72 to help us get a feel for the damage inflation is doing to your retirement and wealth.

Albert Einstein is credited with discovering the Rule of 72, and if you aren't familiar with it, it's time to take notes. This is a concept you need to be familiar with and use on a regular basis to help you see the value of growing your money and protecting it from inflation.

The Rule of 72 shows us the amount of time it takes for your money to double, based on a specific interest rate.

If you're getting 4% on your money, 4% divided into 72 gives you 18. That means your money will double every 18 years.

It's a pretty easy calculation to do and a *very important thing to know.*

The Rule of 72 is a powerful concept because it can work FOR you *or* AGAINST you.

It works *for* when you're growing your money and *against* you when it's being devalued by inflation.

Using the Rule of 72, take the inflation rate of 4% and divide it into 72, and you get 18 years.

This means the value of your money is being cut in half every

18 years.

For example, if you are age 47 and are comfortable living off $100,000 per year when you retire at age 65, that same $100,000 will only buy you a $50,000 lifestyle. Your lifestyle will be cut in half unless you have double the money.

Not a pretty picture!

Now, do you plan on living past age 65? I hope so!

Let's say you live another 18 years and last to age 83. That same $100,000 lifestyle you are living today will be more like a $25,000 lifestyle. Are you comfortable with that? I'm not!

It was SHOCKING to me the first time I saw this.

That's exactly why inflation is such a terrible enemy of wealth and why we must beat it.

$$\frac{18}{4\,\big|\,72}$$

AGE	4% 18 YEARS
29	$ 10,000
47	$ 20,000
65	$ 40,000

We do that by growing our money with a rate of return that outpaces inflation.

Just a small increase in the rate of return on your money can make a dramatic impact on your wealth, thanks to the power of compound interest.

Let's take a newlywed 29-year-old who invests $10,000 at 4% interest. Four divided into 72 is still 18. So his $10,000 is doubling every 18 years and grows to around $40,000 by age 65. Not impressive. Not exciting.

Now he's got a major problem—he's run out of time.

What if instead of getting just 4%, he could have *earned 8%? Would our newly married man now have greater financial independence?*

Of course.

$$\frac{9}{8\sqrt{72}}$$

AGE	8% 9 YEARS
29	$ 10,000
38	$ 20,000
47	$ 40,000
56	$ 80,000
65	$ 160,000

At an interest rate of 8%, your money is doubling every 9 years. That's half the time.

Logically, you might think that doubling the interest rate would double your money, so instead of $40,000, you would end up with $80,000.

But you'd be wrong.

With 8% compounded over 36 years, at age 65, you'll actually have around $160,000!

You've only increased your return from 4% to 8%, but it produced $160,000 vs. $40,000. That's four times more money!

That happens because of the power of compound interest.

Now let's see what would happen if you could get 12% on your money, and it's doubling every 6 years.

This is where it really gets exciting . . .

In 36 years, at age 65, you've got close to *$590,000 vs. $40,000. (You probably expected $640,000, but as interest rates get higher, the Rule of 72 becomes a little less accurate.)*

Even so, isn't the difference in amounts amazing?

The only difference between these is the interest rate.

$$\frac{6}{12\overline{)72}}$$

AGE	12% 6 YEARS
29	$ 10,000
35	$ 20,000
41	$ 40,000
47	$ 77,000
53	$ 152,000
59	$ 300,000
65	$ 590,000

Not more money.

Not more time.

But if you only earn 4%, it just cost you $550,000.

Now you may be asking, how do I grow my money at 8% or 12% in today's market without losing it all when the market tanks?

That's what this book is all about. We'll uncover several strategies we've discovered over the years to outpace inflation and increase your wealth exponentially.

Chapter 3

My Breakup with
Mr. Market

"If I had to give advice, it would be keep out of Wall Street."
— JOHN D. ROCKEFELLER

Ethan Kap wasn't normal.

You could say he had a strange fascination with money. Much more than the average teenager asking for gas money—as a youngster, he had a fascination with the idea that by investing his money, it could automatically grow year after year. It shouldn't have surprised anyone, then, when he bought his very first mutual fund at the age of *fourteen*. In his words…

It was just a normal day at school—until I overheard a conversation that changed my life. Two parents were talking about how anyone can buy stocks and have their money grow larger and larger each year. Some people even became millionaires in the market! Bursting with excitement, I ran home and told my dad that I wanted to invest in the market. I wanted to make millions! I was delighted when he offered to match my $1,500, and together we researched available funds.

With his guidance, I found what I thought was a winner. I invested, watched my money grow over the next five years, and sold at a decent profit.

I was hooked.

Like many people, I bounced from one stock to the next, using one strategy after another like a Las Vegas gambler looking for the big win.

I was convinced I'd found my ticket to riches: Warren Buffett. His stock investment method was simple: He invested in consumer monopolies, or what he called "toll bridges." He did the research and then bought accordingly. He purchased undervalued stocks and held on to them forever— unless the fundamentals of the company changed.

Sounded like a winner to me, so I switched my investing strategy and started buying large blue-chip companies like Coca-Cola, McDonald's, and Colgate. For another five years, I did really great.

You can probably guess what happened next. The stock market crashed.

And because the stock market is no respecter of persons, I — along with everyone else—lost a huge percent of my portfolio in that crash. My dream of watching my dollars multiply had turned into a nightmare.

You may have experienced the sickening, desperate feeling of watching your money evaporate right before your eyes with nothing you can do about it!

If you've ever seen a relationship start with deception or a lie, it usually doesn't turn out too well. No matter the initial strength of the romance, the initial deception or lie will cause one party to lose all trust in the other partner.

I lost my trust in Mr. Market when this happened to me. I still have moments where I think about the potential to make money buying and selling stocks again. But I quickly come back to reality when I think about losing another decade of wealth.

Notable Wall Street Crashes and Recoveries

1901-03
- Fall in the Dow: 46%
- Losses recovered by July 1905
- 2 years to recover

1906-07
- Fall in the Dow: 49%
- Losses recovered by September 1916
- 9 years to recover

1916-17
- Fall in the Dow: 40%
- Losses recovered by November 1919

- 2 years to recover

1919-21
- Fall in the Dow: 47%
- Losses recovered by November 1924
- 3 years to recover

1929-32
- Fall in the Dow: 89%
- Losses recovered by November 1954
- 22 years to recover

1939-42
- Fall in the Dow: 40%
- Losses recovered by
- January 1945
- 3 years to recover

1973-74
- Fall in the Dow: 45%
- Losses recovered by December 1982
- 8 years to recover

I realized that continuing to invest directly in the stock market held no guarantees. I had a goal for growing wealthy, and this wasn't helping me reach that goal. All my savings were in the stock market, and I had no control over how that market performed. In fact, there was a very real risk that I could lose *all my money.*

Can You Afford to Lose Another Decade of Wealth?

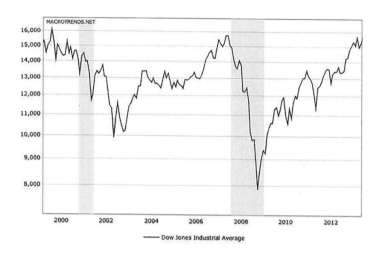

Dow Jones Industrial Average

In September 2013, the Dow Jones Industrial Average hovered at the same level it had 14 years before. Trillions of dollars were lost in stocks, mutual funds, 401(k)s, and other qualified plans. Mr. Market can be extremely rewarding during certain periods but viciously brutal during others. Dreams are crushed, retirements dashed, and plans delayed. Can you really afford to keep rebuilding your wealth every 5 or 10 years?

I live close to Vegas and often take trips down with my family. I am always amazed at the luxurious casinos being built. I hear myself saying, "They can't afford to build these huge casinos by paying out winnings to all the customers."

Most people know the house usually wins, yet thousands of people make the trip and continue gambling away their money.

Sadly, many follow the same pattern regarding their wealth: instead of talking with a trained financial professional, many people put their financial future at risk in the stock market, hoping for that *one* upward swing that will make them extremely wealthy. For those individuals, this can feel like a roller coaster.

I'm sure if someone asked you about taking all their retirement money and gambling it on a roulette wheel, you'd instinctively tell him that's probably not a good idea. Yet that's similar to what people do in the market every day.

It's the difference between the foolish man who built his house upon the sands of risk without talking with a financial professional and the wise man who built his house on a solid financial foundation with the aid of a competent professional. The tide came in and destroyed the man's house on the sand. The man's house on the rock survived and stood strong.

This is exactly why you should seek out good advice so you can know how to PROTECT the PRINCIPAL at all costs.

Take for example, a $100,000 investment. Assume the market drops by 30% and your money goes from $100,000 to $70,000. How much growth do you need just to get back to even? (Hint: it's not 30%.) You'll actually need 42.9% growth on your money to get back to where you started. Now how long does it take to see a 30% loss in the market? It could happen in as little as one year.

And how long does it take to make your money back? Usually, it's not so quick. Let's take a look at some examples in history.[13]

After the great depression, from 1929-32, the Dow fell 89% and took a full 22 years to recover. Now, 22 years until recovery is a bit dramatic so let's look at a few more recent drops.

In 1973-74, the Dow fell by approximately 45%. The losses weren't recovered until December 1982. That means a full 8 years could have passed without folks getting any return on their money.

And, of course, most recently, the crash of 2008. After the market peaked on October 9, 2007, stocks slid downward. By March 5, 2009, the S&P was down 56% and the Dow down 53%. As of this writing, the Dow is still down 3000 points, which is over 21% below where it was 3 years ago. The S&P is still down 24%.

Wall Street seems to have convinced many people that it's necessary to forgo guaranteed returns and risk principal, in favor of *possible* 8, 10, or even 12% return on their investments.

Wall Street's favorite tool could be considered a financial calculator showing how much money we'll have in retirement if our money grows at 12 or even 15%!

But often, those illustrations leave out several major factors like market downturns, taxes, and fees.

Unfortunately, due to recent events, we know all too well that even after all the worry, investigation, and research, the gains we've had in our retirement—even after years of growth—can be wiped out with a market downturn.

According to the DALBAR Report

"For the 20 years ending December 31, 2019, the S&P 500 Index averaged 6.06% a year. The average equity fund investor earned a market return of only 4.25%"

DALBAR INC, 2020 QAIB Report

In just one year, during the great recession of 2008, the Dow Jones Industrial lost 1/3 of its value!

More than a few Americans saw their retirement dreams destroyed right before their eyes as their nest egg dropped. But, unfortunately, they were powerless to do anything about it.

In addition, DALBAR Inc. (the nation's leading financial services market research firm) shows that the average investor outpaced inflation by just 1.44% over the past several years.

But that's not the story we want to hear. Instead, we want to hear about great rates of return. People love to talk about a new hot stock or the latest news on a new tech company that could give them a great rate of return. But let's take a closer look.

In our example, Joe starts with $10,000 and gets a 100% rate of return in year one, bouncing his balance up to $20,000.

The next year the market drops by 50%, leaving him with $10,000 again. In year three, it goes up again by 100% to $20,000. Then drops again in the fourth year by 50%, setting him right back at $10,000.

Year	Market	Starting Balance	Ending Balance
1	+100%	10,000	20,000
2	-50%	20,000	10,000
3	+100%	10,000	20,000
4	-50%	20,000	10,000

In this case, the market did average a 25% rate of return. But how much additional cash does Joe have left to show for his 25% average rate of return?

Zero.

Even though brokers quote stats about great rates of return in the market, investors could still be netting absolutely zero.

Take that same $10,000, compound it monthly for four years at 6.5% without it being subject to market volatility, and you could end up with $12,960.20.

A 25% return in the market gave Joe $10,000, but a much lower 6.5% rate, compounded every year, would give him almost $13,000. It's easy to see why people are getting confused about where they should put their money.

Rub Some Salt in the Wound

It's not just market dips that can negatively affect your principal. It's also fees. Often 401(k)'s, mutual funds, other stock market-related investments, as well as non-investment tools like life insurance, annuities, and others, come with fees—fees many people don't understand because they can be very confusing.

This 1-3% fee structure compounded over time can mean the difference between a comfortable retirement and having to watch every penny. Even if you realize a 10% return in the market, it could end up 7-8% after fees.

Even a 1%-point difference in fees can have a big impact. For example, let's take a 35-year-old worker who leaves $20,000 in his 401(k) plan when he switches jobs and never adds to that account. If the account earned 7% a year, minus 0.5% in annual fees, his balance would only grow to about $139,836 at retirement. But if the fees were 1.5% annually, the average net return would be reduced to 5.5%, and the $20,000 would grow to about $103,747. Thus, over 30 years, the 1% increase in fees whittles down the account balance by over 26%.[14] Even worse, when you tack on fees while you are losing money, it can be very difficult to regain the ground you've lost so you can start making progress again.

You Can't Grow Your Money If It's Shrinking

When I went back to the drawing board for the last time, I didn't listen to what everyone else was doing. I made a list of what *I* needed. I needed a way to save my money and build financial independence that was simple, easy to follow, and protected from market crashes—a way that *guaranteed* growth. But that's not all. It also needed to provide good tax benefits because taxes can affect your wealth if you aren't careful. Oh, and wait—I needed to be able to access my money at any time; without getting charged excessive fees and penalties as you would with other plans.

I'm happy to say I found the perfect solution. It's not a get-rich-quick scheme. But it's also not gambling with my future. I'm not the only one who's had a bad experience in the market. In fact, many people have been looking for an alternative. But many don't know where to look. They are fearful of making a wrong decision and losing even more.

The Wrap

When you start down the Crash Proof Wealth path, you'll give yourself permission; permission to reevaluate old ideas and consider alternative ways to become wealthy. Remember, there is risk in whatever you do. This is your hard-earned money, and you should talk with a financial professional to choose the best place for it. Also, give yourself permission to grow wealthy while protecting against some of the other enemies of wealth.

There is good news. There are alternate solutions. The pathway of the wealthy is simple and proven, although it may not be easy. Soon you will have a clear plan to help supplement the conventional wisdom, with a proven solution that can help give you relief, hope, and faith in your future.

With this book and the help of your financial professional, you will have the blueprint you need to make the moves that can protect your life, family, and finances by creating a rock on which you can build a financial foundation that you can count on.

Section 2

ACCEPTING
A NEW REALITY

"I must create a system or be enslaved by another man's."

— WILLIAM BLAKE

"Reasonable people adapt themselves to the world.
Unreasonable people attempt to adapt the world to themselves.
All progress, therefore, depends on unreasonable people."

— GEORGE BERNARD SHAW

Chapter 4

Microwave Money and Pop Culture Gurus

"There are as many opinions as there are experts."
— Franklin D. Roosevelt

"Even when the experts all agree, they may well be mistaken."
— Bertrand Russell

"Bear Stearns is not in trouble!"

"I believe in the Bear Stearns Franchise, and at 69 bucks, I'm not giving up on the thing!"

These statements were both made by Jim Cramer of Mad Money CNBC, uttered on March 6th and March 11th, 2008.

Eleven days later, Bear Stearns' stock had dropped from $69.00 to $2.00.

Who controls the financial education most people get these days? Think for a second about who most people are listening to. You may have read articles from pop culture money magazines. You might have followed the popular TV personalities or read their books. You may have listened to the HR department at work suggesting you invest in the 401(k) because you'll get matching funds! Free money!

Wait just a minute. Did you know that the 401(k) and other qualified retirement programs are trillion-dollar businesses? By some estimates, there are between 7 and 11 trillion dollars in qualified plans. That's a lot of money to trust to anyone.

The bottom line is that a 401(k) might be smart for a portion of your money to take advantage of tax breaks today. At the same time, for another portion of your money, it might make sense to diversify outside Wall Street by paying the tax today and potentially avoiding future tax increases.

Do They Practice What They Preach?

Almost everybody's heard of—if not listened to—Suze Orman, the personal finance expert. Orman hosts her own show, has written a handful of bestsellers, and was named by *Time* magazine as one of the world's one hundred most influential people. She encourages viewers, listeners, and readers to buy term and invest the difference in mutual funds.

But does she practice what she preaches?

She estimates her liquid net worth at about $25 million, with an additional $7 million in houses. Where is the majority of her money invested?

"I save it and build it in municipal bonds. I buy zero-coupon municipal bonds, and all the bonds I buy are triple-A-rated and insured, so even if the city goes under, I get my money." Orman quips.[37]

Doesn't sound like *she* has the majority of her money in the market, does it? That's a Crash Proof Wealth strategy if I've ever heard one.

When asked about playing the stock market, she says that "I have a million dollars in the stock market, because if I lose a million dollars, I don't personally care."[37] In short, the financial guru coaching the American public has a portfolio few could live with.

Maybe someone who can afford to lose $1 million has no qualms about encouraging other people to invest in the market, too.

Of course, it probably doesn't help that one of her personal sponsors is TD Ameritrade. TD Ameritrade is a company that makes money facilitating stock trades. Suze Orman is often seen on advertisements encouraging people to open up an account with TD Ameritrade. Now, does Orman's advice to buy term and invest the difference in the market sound fishy to you?

Then, of course, there's Jim Cramer, investment guru and host of CNBC's *Mad Money*, who advises that people invest their mad money—or in other words, non-retirement funds—in the stock market. Cramer regularly makes recommendations not only to his own show's viewers but also to the audience of NBC's *Today*

Show, steering people to the market buys he thinks will pay off handsomely.

How's that been working?

Not so well, according to news reports. As one example, reported by the *Wall Street Cheat Sheet*, Cramer recommended that viewers buy CIT Group, a stock he said was primed for upside. Fewer than four weeks later, CIT filed for bankruptcy. The *Cheat Sheet's* assessment? "This type of incredibly speculative advice is as radioactive to the general investing public as a post-nuclear explosion site… If 'In Cramer You Trust,' (like the CNBC commercials tell you to do), you are probably going to have lost over 90% of your investment by the open on Monday."[15]

Summing it all up, a report in *Baron's* stated that, "Cramer is wildly inconsistent, and the performance of individual picks varies widely. So widely, in fact, that it is impossible to know with confidence that any sample of Cramer's recommendations will enable you to outperform the market."[16]

These are just two examples of the media promoting the Wall Street conventional wisdom—that has a questionable (at best) track record of success and often proves just the opposite! In fact, they've done such a good job convincing Americans of the conventional financial wisdom of investing in stock, maxing out 401(k)s, buying term and then investing the difference, that we've seen people lose by following each other like sheep right off the financial cliff.[17]

Those who grow wealthy outside the stock market, we feel, are building their house on a solid foundation. For example, part of that solid foundation is using an alternate solution like having a properly structured cash value life insurance policy with a death benefit to manage risk, creating the potential for cash value accumulation to supplement future financial needs and help diversify taxes.

Contractors don't put buildings on foundations of clay or sand. They use concrete. Why then would we be any less careful with our entire financial future? The solid foundation we are talking about is safer places to save money. It's the safety net you can count on in good times and bad.

People who have their money outside of Wall Street don't worry about market volatility. They have their foundation growing using an alternative solution, plus, they give themselves many other living benefits. We'll get to those shortly.

The Wrap

So far on our Crash Proof Wealth path, we've covered three critical topics:

1. Several people feel the Wall Street conventional financial wisdom has failed many Americans. It's time to leave the status quo behind.

2. Investing in the market holds no guarantees. It is more
    like building your financial house on a foundation of
    sand.

3. Pop culture financial gurus get paid to fill airtime, not
    make you wealthy. Some feel that following their advice
    can cost you big time.

But the fun doesn't end there. There's another force we have to
contend with. An extraordinary story about a bank robber named
Willie Sutton might shed some light on it for you.

Chapter 5

THE WILLIE SUTTON SLAP DOWN

*"In this world nothing can be said to be
certain, except death and taxes."*
—BENJAMIN FRANKLIN

Willie Sutton wasn't born a bank robber.

Willie was the fourth of five children born to an ordinary
Brooklyn family on June 30, 1901. Like all the other kids in
Brooklyn, he went to school. But he didn't stick with it very long.
Filled with dreams, he left home after the eighth grade in search
of fame and fortune.

But Willie had a problem. He loved expensive clothes and
the finer things of life—things that were hard to finance on the
meager wages he brought in from his string of menial jobs like
gardening, clerking, and drilling. Never satisfied, he jumped from
one job to another with alarming frequency. His longest period of
continuous employment was 18 months.

At the age of 28, he got married. But his wedded bliss was
short-lived because his wife divorced him when he landed in jail.
You see, Willie Sutton had finally found a career that offered fatter

paychecks, albeit riskier working conditions. Willie Sutton was a bank robber.

After serving a brief stint, Willie was back on the streets and back at his lucrative profession. According to the FBI, Willie Sutton mastered the art of disguise—a talent that earned him the nickname "The Actor." He attempted to rob the Corn Exchange Bank and Trust Company in Philadelphia, Pennsylvania disguised as a mailman. The curiosity of a passerby derailed his plans. (Not to worry, he returned to the same bank less than a year later, and this time was successful.) At other times, he disguised himself as a messenger, policeman, or maintenance man. He pulled off a sizable heist at a Broadway jewelry store in broad daylight by disguising himself as a telegraph messenger.

In addition to his innovative disguises, Willie was distinguished from other bank robbers by his gentle demeanor. Victims of his robberies and innocent bystanders in the teller lines reported how polite he was. Many commented that he behaved like a real gentleman. One victim quipped that witnessing a Willie Sutton robbery was like being at the movies, except the usher had a gun.

In June 1931, Willie's luck ran out—sort of. He was charged with assault and robbery, found guilty, and sentenced to 30 years in prison. But again, that 18-month charm kicked in. 18 months after he was incarcerated, just in time to celebrate Christmas in 1932, Willie roped two nine-foot sections of ladder together and scaled up and over the prison wall.

On February 5, 1934, Willie returned to the Corn Exchange Bank and Trust Company, this time with a machine gun. Things didn't go so well. He was apprehended and sentenced to serve 25 to 50 years in the Eastern State Penitentiary in Philadelphia.

Fast-forward to April 3, 1945. Willie Sutton was one of 12 convicts who burrowed out of the penitentiary through a tunnel his *fifth* escape attempt from the same prison. Philadelphia police officers recaptured him the same day. He was tossed back in prison, this time for life as a fourth-time offender. Just to be on the safe side, officials transferred him to the Philadelphia County Prison in Holmesburg, Pennsylvania, away from the prison where he'd practiced so many escapes.

Willie lasted almost two years at Holmesburg before he and a group of other prisoners dressed up as prison guards, sashayed across the prison yard after dark and carried two ladders to the prison wall. Caught in the beams of the prison searchlight, Willie Sutton flashed a grin and yelled, "It's okay," and kept moving with his plan. No one stopped him. He was free again.

On March 20, 1950, a little more than three years after he walked away from Holmesburg, Willie Sutton was added to the FBI list of Ten Most Wanted Fugitives. In addition to distributing his poster to police departments throughout the nation, the FBI also gave his photograph to tailors. After all, this was a man who dressed impeccably in expensive, tailored clothing. Two years later, Willie was nonchalantly riding a New York City subway when a twenty-four-year-old tailor's son recognized him as the man from the wanted posters. He quietly followed Willie to a gas station and watched him buy a battery for his car before he called the police with the tip.

Face-to-face with New York's finest, Willie didn't resist arrest. But he also didn't fess up to any robberies or any other crimes, for that matter. He was hauled into Queens County Court, where he was sentenced to an additional 30 years to life. It was a drop in the bucket. Willie already owed one life sentence plus 105 years. They tossed him into a cell at Attica State Prison and threw away the key. If all went according to plan, he'd never see daylight again.

Of course, that wasn't the end of the story. Seventeen years later, the system took pity on Willie. He was seriously ill with emphysema and needed major surgery on the arteries in both his legs. On Christmas Eve of 1969, the State of New York released Willie Sutton from prison. He was sixty-eight. Just two years later, in an irony that's stranger than fiction, Willie did a television commercial to promote the new photo credit card for what else - a Connecticut bank.

Willie Sutton died November 2, 1980, at the age of 79. Before he died, he authored two books about his illustrious career as a bank robber. When asked why he robbed banks, he smiled and replied, "Because that's where the money is." [18]

Willie Sutton's Law

Why did Willie rob banks? Willie said it best himself: he robbed banks because that's where the money was. Wherever wealth is accumulated, someone will always try to take it. In some circles, this type of human behavior is called "Willie Sutton's Law."

If you are like most Americans, you may feel you are living Willie Sutton's Law every day. Shallow bank balances, high expenses, and credit card statements and bills on the counter make us feel as though someone is constantly trying to take our money away!

But before you sell the car, cut up the credit cards, and stop buying food for the dog, let's take a better look at exactly who might be trying to rob you. The following tactics are completely legal, and unless you are aware, you might not even see them coming.

Who is the modern-day Willie Sutton imposter? It is the Tax Man.

But wait! Shouldn't we all share the cost of doing business in this country by sharing the costs of education, paving roads, and running the government? Sure—that was the idea. But if you're not careful, and if you invest in qualified retirement plans, you may one day have to pay deferred taxes and witness a sickening scene unfold. You could end up losing some of your retirement to taxes, perhaps much more than you bargained for. There's an alternate legal and ethical way to prevent that, and you'll be excited when you see how simple it is to accomplish.

You are probably aware that, depending on your tax bracket, the Tax Man could be grabbing up to 20-30% of your paycheck every pay period. (Did you know that Thomas Jefferson said that an income tax of even 1% is equivalent to slavery?) Wait a minute. Wasn't it you that commuted in rush hour traffic, dealt with upset customers, and missed out on the kids' baseball games while working those 50+ hour weeks? You do all the work, yet the Tax Man always takes his cut.

But income tax is just the beginning, the proverbial tip of the iceberg. Take a second and think of all the other taxes you might be paying: state income tax, social security tax, property tax, Medicare tax, phone tax, utility tax, sales tax, gasoline tax, and vehicle tax—not just on the purchase, but also on the annual registration. And in the next few years, we could be looking at unprecedented levels of healthcare taxes.[19] In fact, almost every transaction you make is taxed.

Consider your average morning. Almost every time you brush your teeth, turn on a light, eat a bowl of cereal, use the phone or access the Internet, taxes take a bite.

When you get in your car, drive down the road, go out to lunch, or even take out the trash, the Tax Man is right there in the shadows, like Willie Sutton, to take your money. It's enough to drive you crazy. So, doesn't it seem sheer lunacy, then, to pay even more taxes on the money you save for retirement?

The Trillion Dollar Tax Target

Hey, wait a minute! Hasn't the government established tax-deferred programs to help people save and invest for retirement *without* paying taxes up front? Indeed, but remember Willie Sutton's Law? Wherever wealth is accumulated, someone will want to come and take it.

Do you have any idea how much wealth is accumulated in government-sponsored qualified retirement plans like IRAs and 401(k)s?

Trillions of dollars

If you aren't careful, the profits of these plans could end up largely being Uncle Sam's. Here's why. Imagine for just a minute that you're a farmer. You purchase a bag of corn seed. As the sun begins to dip below the horizon on that late spring evening, you gaze out over your fields, filled with the anticipation of an abundant harvest following months of sustained labor.

As time goes by, you do everything right. You fertilize, water, weed, tend, and protect. Then, it's harvest time at last, and the abundance you imagined is realized ten times over. You're filled with the satisfaction of a job well done as you watch a convoy of trucks taking your crops to market.

As the last trailer disappears from sight, a shiny sedan roars up, tires crunching in the gravel at the edge of the road. Out hops a well-dressed man. As you remove your hat and wipe your well-worn sleeve across your dampened brow, he opens a notebook and stands with ballpoint pen ready. Without so much as an introduction because, really, he doesn't need one, he poses the question: So, farmer, you have two options. Do you want to pay taxes on that bag of seed you hauled in here last spring or on the five trucks of crops you just sent to market?

He's kidding, right?

No. He's not. Let's pretend you, the farmer, had a choice: you can pay taxes on the seed the money you start out with, or you can pay taxes on the crop, which represents the increase that grew from your initial seed money.

In the government-sponsored, tax-deferred retirement plans, you pay taxes on any increase. You're paying taxes on the truckloads of crops. With the approach we'll show you, you pay taxes on the seed. The crops are yours, and you get to keep all the money you grow.

To help you more clearly understand how this works, let's look at some actual figures.

Option 1: A post-tax plan like a Roth IRA

Invest $5,000 a year for 30 years.

Total of $150,000.

In a 33% tax bracket, you pay $49,500 in taxes on that money as you earn it over the 30 years.

Assume you experience a 6.5% growth rate on that money. By the end of the 30 years, you'll have $333,903.28 in your account.

Option 2: A tax-deferred plan like a 401(k)

Invest $5,000 a year in the stock market for 30 years. Growth rate: 6.5%

Total of $498,363.11.

You didn't pay taxes up front on this money, so you've now got more money. Okay, you're probably thinking, this is a no-brainer—I'll take the tax-deferred plan with the bigger balance!

But wait: remember taxes are due? How much of that $498,363.11 belongs to Uncle Sam? You have $498,363.11 in your retirement account. Let's say you take out $73,000 a year to live on during retirement. You can take $73,000 a year out of your account for nine years before your money is gone (assuming it's still growing at 6.5%). On that $73,000 each year, you now have to pay taxes on the "crop" (assuming you are in the same 33% tax bracket). Thus, you will pay $24,090 in taxes every year. In nine years, you will have paid $216,810 in taxes.

Remember how much you saved by deferring taxes—by waiting to pay on the crop instead of on the seed? You saved $49,500. That means you will have paid Uncle Sam back everything you saved in just the first two and a half years. In the next six and a half years, you will pay an additional $167,310 in taxes on your harvest.

In fact, according to Scott Shultz, you could end up paying up to five times more taxes using a qualified plan like a 401(k) than you saved during your entire working years.[20]

Now ask yourself that question again: Would I rather pay taxes on my seed or on my crop?

Conventional wisdom says you'll be in a lower tax bracket when you retire, so deferring taxes is a good thing. Not so fast. In later years, people often lose deductions because kids move out and mortgages are paid off.

Plus, do you know what the tax rates are going to be when you retire? How does the Federal Government plan to pay back the trillion-dollar deficit? None of us, not even the most seasoned prognosticator, can predict where taxes will be when you retire. But a quick look back into history shows the top tax brackets have been as high as 94%.

This rate was for those who made $200k or more from 1944 to 1945. If this rate was still the top rate in 2009 and adjusting for inflation, it would affect those who made $2.4 million in 2009. On a similar note, those making $10,001 from 1944 to 1945 would have to pay 41%. Again, adjusting for inflation, it would be equivalent for those who made $127,553 in 2009. Those rates are still higher than the current top tax rate, which at the time of the writing of this book is 39.6%.[38]

The good news is that you don't have to pay on your crop. We'll show you how to pay on your seed so you can enjoy your full harvest. By paying on your seed, you are still meeting your tax obligation. Paying tax on the seed gives you major tax advantages on your growth while at the same time protecting the principal from volatility in the market. When structured and funded properly, you could have access to your money throughout your life. It also allows you to transfer your wealth to your heirs without them having to pay income tax on that money.

The Crash Proof Wealth path is not just about keeping your money protected from market volatility. It's about incorporating available resources to assist you in protecting your money from all the enemies of wealth.

But it doesn't end there. It gives you another arrow in your arsenal to defeat another foe: the interest vampire.

Chapter 6

Killing the Interest Vampire

*"There are two types of people in the world. Those
who pay interest and those who EARN it."*
—Unknown

*"The rich rule over the poor, and the
borrower is servant to the lender."*
—Proverbs 22:7

*"Banks don't lend their money. They lend the
money somebody else left there."*
—Adam Smith

I was shocked when I awoke from my zombie-like state.

Much like you, my day was pretty routine. I woke up, went to work, came home, saw the family, ate dinner, went to sleep, and did it all over again the next morning. Every two weeks, the paycheck came in. It immediately disappeared going to mortgage payments, car payments, credit card payments, and other expenses.

At the end of the month, I had worked hard. But I had little to show for it. I was a member of the financial living dead by going through the motions to pay everyone else, but not myself.

Like most Americans, I had the financial life sucked right out of me by the vampire of interest.

How would you like a 34% raise? Of course, you would.

If you're an average American, you could be paying a whopping 34% of your after-tax income in interest.[21]

Take out a twenty from your wallet, rip a 1/3 of it off, and that's about how much of your after-tax income could be going to interest every year.

You might be saying to yourself, I shop really hard for good interest rates. I check not only the price of what I'm buying, but I also work hard to keep my credit score high so I can get a good interest rate on my purchases.

Price and *interest rate* are the two factors everyone focuses on—but they're not the things that kill you. The killer is the *volume* of interest.

Imagine buying a car for $30,000, getting a five-year loan with an interest rate of 7.5%. How much will you pay in interest over the life of that loan? Easy, you say, whipping out your calculator: 7.5% of $30,000 is $2,250.

Wise Money Alert

Your 7.5% car loan could end up costing you more like 20.2% by the time you pay off that loan!

Right?

Wrong! You'll actually pay more than twice that much. The amount of interest you will pay on that $30,000 car loan could be up to $6,068.31—20.2% of the amount you borrowed.

Wait! How is that possible?

It happens because of three letters that follow your interest rate quote: APR or annual percentage rate. The 7.5% is the rate you pay on the balance of the loan every year. So by the time you are done paying off your car loan, you'll have paid over 20% on that loan, not just 7.5%!

Here's where the volume of interest comes in. Let's say, over the course of your lifetime, you finance 10 cars at $30,000 each. That's a total of $300,000.

Assuming you get the same 7.5% interest on those loans, that means you'll pay about $6,000 in interest on each loan or $60,000 in interest on your 10 cars. I don't know about you, but I think $60,000 is a big deal. A really big deal, especially when current figures reveal that the average American reaches retirement age with only $88,000 in savings. That means you will have dumped out, in interest on cars, almost as much as most people save for their entire retirement. (We won't even cover leasing here. Leasing cars can often turn out to be even worse than traditional financing.)

Wise Money Alert

If you thought interest on cars was hard to swallow, this might really make you sick.

Home loans are front-loaded, with most of the interest paid in the first years of the loan.

Because of how often people refinance homes, over 10 or 20 years of paying down mortgages, up to 86% of every dollar you pay on your mortgage could be going straight to interest!

With purchase price and interest combined on your 10 cars, even if you keep them until they're paid off, you will have kissed away $360,000 on vehicles. We're talking a total of *four times* what many people save for their retirement.

What if you could keep the majority of that $360,000 flowing back into YOUR pocket instead of some lender or car company?

You can.

I'll introduce you to this great financial tool and multiple others. Let's get started.

BUILDING ON A STRONG FOUNDATION

"Do you wish to rise? Begin by descending. You plan a tower that will pierce the clouds? Lay first the foundation."

— Saint Augustine

Chapter 7

DEFEATING THE ENEMIES OF WEALTH

"Wherever wealth is accumulated someone
will be there to try and steal it."
—R. NELSON NASH

Jason Smith slid into the front seat, slammed the door, and slumped forward until his forehead pressed against the steering wheel. His stomach was in knots, and a dull ache throbbed behind his temples. Another roller coaster week in the market had dropped his 401(k) value substantially.

He dreaded facing Susan. After all, it had been *his* idea to max out the 401(k). She'd wanted to keep their contributions smaller—to put some of Jason's salary in a conventional savings account or maybe some short-term CDs. She worried about emergencies and about covering the kids' college expenses—all arguments that he disregarded at the time.

He'd read some articles written by the industry's top gurus—and he figured he knew what he was doing. He knew that the 401(k) was the most popular retirement plan in America. He not only wanted all the free money he could get through his employer's match, but he'd heard about the great tax savings to be had from socking the maximum amount possible into a 401(k). All the other guys in his department were doing it, and they seemed savvy enough.

Jason had won out, and for the past six years, a large percentage of every paycheck had gone to his 401(k) account. It had seemed like a good idea at the time. But that was *before.*

Before the market experienced a nearly unprecedented downturn that reduced the value of mutual funds and retirement accounts of people all over the country.

Before he'd found out how he had not known this? The money in his 401(k) might as well have been locked up in Fort Knox because it was a major pain to get at any of it.

After all, it was *his* money. And he needed some of it.

And now—easing reluctantly up the driveway—Jason knew that what had seemed like such a good idea six years ago was turning out to be an emotional and financial rollercoaster with more downs than ups.

Jason sunk into the sofa in the living room and proceeded to tell Susan the bad news. Another drop in economic forecasts had caused a major drop in the market, costing them thousands with every drop. First off, his account was not even worth *half* of what he thought it was. His hard-earned money was gone thanks to the volatility of a market over which he had no control. So much for his dream of retiring with millions.

Second, Susan had really wanted to access some money for the kitchen remodel they badly needed. If he took the money out, he'd be slapped with so many fees and penalties—including a tax penalty—that he'd scarcely break even.

Even if he decided to brave the penalties, he'd lose a fortune selling the funds in his account when the market was so low. He would kiss away what hadn't already been lost to the market crash.

Finally, he didn't even dare borrow from his account. That little carrot that had been dangled in front of his nose six years ago turned out to have a very painful string attached. What they hadn't told Jason when he invested in a 401(k) was that if he lost his job, the loan would be due in full, usually within two months' time.

With a rumored corporate merger in the works that could result in potential layoffs, that was a chance Jason couldn't afford to take.

Maxing out the 401(k) is not the best idea, Jason sheepishly admitted.

A few days later, after a few emails between friends, Jason got a link to a website that helped him figure out when he would run out of money in retirement. He was intrigued.

It would tell him how long his retirement savings would last. So he started punching in numbers, thinking things couldn't possibly get worse, and while he was a bit shocked at what he saw, he also got some good news.

The bad news: Jason Smith would run out of money at age 71.

Simply put, based on his current plan and the income he felt he would need during retirement, he would only have enough income till he reached age 71.

Seventy-one? Jason wondered what he would do then!

As visions of greeting customers at the local warehouse store clouded his thoughts, he noticed the website offered a way out, and it could all be explained by an insurance professional. Let's just say it was a hard sell for Susan. We can imagine why she might be just a little skeptical about Jason's financial know-how right about now.

Reluctantly, Susan agreed, and Jason called to schedule an appointment with a professional insurance agent. They had a short 20-minute conversation with Michael. At the end of the conversation, he offered them a customized blueprint to help them grow their money outside the stock market with major tax advantages. He offered to show them how the entire process works in black and white right from their own computer. Michael is one of the few professionals specifically trained to implement these solutions, so he uses the phone and internet to help people all across the country.

It was done using a 100-year-old proven strategy for keeping money growing outside Wall Street. It came with the potential for growth if the markets went up and with complete downside protection, although you would still have to pay fees and the cost of insurance. If structured and funded properly, it could also give you the ability to access your cash value throughout your life. In fact, that was one of the major benefits—that you could use it to Finance Yourself to Wealth™. Meaning you could borrow against your cash value for major purchases like cars, college tuition, or vacations and then pay your loan back to yourself while the cash continued to grow as if you hadn't touched it. Of course, it would be important to have other long-term savings in case of an emergency. Jason was particularly intrigued by that idea. Ultimately, it was a way to possibly reduce the amount of interest he would pay to banks or with credit card companies!

Let's take a break in the story and get a few of the basics out of the way while we're waiting for Michael to call. Because whether you have a 401(k) or not, this will be new information. And like GI Joe says, "Knowing is half the battle." And, again, you should talk with a qualified financial professional for more details about this and other strategies mentioned to better understand if they are suitable for your situation.

You might have assumed, just like our friend Jason, that a 401(k) or mutual fund was a solid way to save for retirement. After all, that's what many of the pop culture gurus advocate. So, right out of the gate, let's see what one financial analyst had to say about it:

The American public has been hoodwinked by political and corporate forces into relying on the 401(k) as the primary long-term investment mechanism. In doing so, the stock market has been put at center stage in providing for a comfortable retirement for the average American. The 401(k) represents an implicit promise to middle-class Americans that they can live off the income that they receive from stock ownership, just like the rich do. It is a promise impossible to fulfill; it is the great 401(k) hoax.[22]

Hoax sounds like a pretty strong word, but that's potentially what the 401(k) plan is.

Here's a quick crash course on 401(k) plans. Money in a 401(k) is often invested in stocks and mutual funds. If the market goes up, so can your money. If you have money in a 401(k) with stocks or mutual funds, your money could be at risk for loss as well!

That means if the market goes down, you can lose. Lastly, your 401(k) contributions are made *before* you pay taxes on the money, so you're taxed as you withdraw money from the plan. (Here's where you see that you are being taxed on the crop, not the seed.) And don't forget, your money could be tied up until you retire unless you want to pay the penalties and taxes on an early withdrawal.

Now, let's get back to Michael.

It's 5 pm on Thursday evening, and Jason and Susan are sitting in front of the computer when Michael calls. Jason is all ears. But Susan, feeling like she's just had the proverbial blanket yanked out from under her feet with the 401(k) debacle, is hanging back. Still skeptical, she goes for the jugular with this comment:

"I need to ask something, right up front," she says. Michael welcomes the question. After detailing what had just happened with their 401(k), Susan squares herself up in her chair. "We've listened to other financial gurus and advisors, and it's gotten us where we are now. Why should we listen to you?" she asks.

"I understand your skepticism in talking with another financial professional. The difference is, I'm focused on alternative strategies. I help people build a strong foundation so [that] my clients don't experience a negative crediting on money in market downturns. They would still have to pay fees and the cost of insurance. 401(k) plans or mutual funds can be the *risky* for the bulk or all of your money, as the market can have volatility" Michael explains. "In fact, depending on how you direct your contributions, it could put your entire retirement principal at risk." Susan, clearly frustrated, glares at Jason.

"Tonight, I'm going to talk to you about some of the biggest enemies of building wealth and also about how you can start on the path to becoming a wealthy outside Wall Street.

A couple of the threats that we must protect against to build wealth are, 1) the actual loss of your money in the market (once you lose money, it can take a substantial amount of time to make it up), 2) taxes, and 3) interest. Many folks don't know it, but they could be paying up to one-third of every dollar they make toward interest of some sort. This is essentially making them employees of the tax man and the lenders at the same time."

"Let's talk about putting your money at risk for loss. To begin, let's look at how your mutual fund or stock performs. How much money you end up with for retirement usually depends completely on the market," Michael explains. "The market is uncertain; it can go up, it can go down, or it can stay flat and completely out of your control. So, your future is tied to how well the market cooperates, without any input from you."

While Jason and Susan tried to wrap their heads around that piece of information, Michael started asking some pretty tough questions. "Jason, how much do you really know about your 401(k)?"

"Clearly not as much as I thought I did," Jason mumbles.

"Well, let's start with your 401(k) manager—do you even know who it is?" Jason shakes his head, and Michael goes on. "Do you know what funds you're invested in or even what companies your funds invest in? Most people enrolled in 401(k) plans can't even list the funds or companies in which they are investing. That's risky business."

"Interesting," Susan smugly replies. "That sounds more like *gambling* to me."

"There's more," Michael says. "I know that you've already found out about some of the tax implications. Think about this: if you don't like paying taxes right now, what makes you think you're going to like it any better 20 years from now? When you start to withdraw your 401(k) money for retirement, you're going to have to pay taxes on it. That means if you're in a 28% tax bracket, you could have about one-third less actual money than you have in your account."

(A quick tip: in a 401(k) plan, you'll be paying taxes on the crop, not the seed. And this is called tax savings? What an irony. People invest in a 401(k) plan to save taxes today, but in reality, they could end up actually paying *more* taxes when they retire—not only because they're paying on the crop, but because they could potentially be in a higher tax bracket when they begin taking distributions from their 401(k) plans.)

"You've got three children, right?" Michael asks. Susan says, "yes." "If you don't manage to use up your 401(k) during your retirement, it will be passed on to your heirs. Not only could they face income tax on the money they receive from your 401(k), but they could have to pay estate taxes as well.

There's another issue with a 401(k) plan you need to be aware of—fees. Many folks don't know how much in fees they are really paying. Unfortunately, it can add up to a substantial sum, and the fund managers always get paid whether your money grows or not."

Jason slaps his palm against the table. "I feel like I've been misled!" he cries. "Our HR guy pushed a bunch of papers in front of me and encouraged me to sign on the dotted line, all the while touting matching funds and company support. But he never said anything about getting out! All the gurus on TV, and everyone else for that matter, say to max out my 401(k).

Susan clears her throat loudly. "Oh, yeah, well—everyone except Susan," Jason admits.

Now, both Jason and Susan are ready to listen to Michael. He's shown them why the old way wasn't working. Jason feels like he's learned more about the 401(k) program in the last 20 minutes than in the previous two decades.

Susan, who has softened a little toward Jason says, "I'm feeling ripped off, too. Just yesterday, I read a column by a well-respected financial guru. Her advice was to buy term and invest the difference in mutual funds. It's ironic that she was the spokesperson for TD Ameritrade!"

Jason chuckles. "Yeah, we've both seen the results of those."

How efficient do you think the average business would be if it suffered constant turnover—in other words, if new people came in on a regular basis, bringing new ideas and new ways of doing things? Well, that's what happens with mutual funds—except instead of people, the turnover involves stocks (in other words, excessive trading in the portfolio). Mutual fund managers are constantly changing the stocks in the portfolio. (Translation: you never know from one day to the next exactly *what's* in your portfolio.)

In the 1950s, the average portfolio turnover rate was about 15%. Today, 100% turnover is commonplace, and as much as 300% turnover is typical. Just a few years ago, *Forbes* magazine reported turnover rates so high that even the reporter was astonished. Rates ranged from 523% to a staggering 827%. The result of all these turnovers is that the cost of doing business for mutual funds has doubled since the 1950s, instead of going down. And who pays for the increased cost? That's right: the investors. Lucky dogs.[23]

"We all watched as the market toppled," says Michael, "taking with it the retirement dreams of many Americans. Even those who had enjoyed growth watched as the value of their nest eggs were nearly half their previous value. And they felt powerless to do anything about it. But, you know what?" Michael continues, "Even without the correction we recently witnessed, there are always ups and downs that we can't control. Studies have shown that over the past 180 years that the average market return after factoring for inflation is as low as 1.2%."[24]

"Here's what it amounts to," Michael says. "As an investor, you put up 100% of the money, and you take 100% of the risk. *You're* the one whose principal is on the line. This is fine if you have money you can stand to lose, but this is NOT the way that that savvy investors live. They build a solid foundation and protect the principal."

"Yeah, I found the site because a friend referred it to me. I liked what I read there. It was really eye-opening. I felt like it was time to try a different approach."

Susan interjects, "The Crash Proof Wealth program sounds good to me."

"It does make sense," Jason agrees. "But I'm not sure what to do at this point. I feel stuck in my 401(k), which I can't get out of, and I'm not thinking I can afford any mutual funds for a while — at least not until we pull out of the hole we're in. So, what do we do now?"

Michaels laughs and says to Jason, "Jason, I've got great news for you."

"It's about time I got some *good* news for a change!" Jason laughs.

"You're a whole lot better informed now than before our meeting," Michael points out. "And now I'm going to show you a couple of alternate solutions and how you *can* get on the right track, starting today. Regardless of your situation with the 401(k), I think we'll find some good solutions together. "I'm going to show you multiple strategies that will keep your money out of the market and offer other strategies that allow you to Finance Yourself to Wealth™ and receive interest that builds cash value based on the performance of the underlying index. You could better manage the amount you pay in interest to banks and credit card companies, plus, have access to your cash value throughout your life. Sound good?"

Jason looks like he's about to cry again—this time from relief.

Chapter 8

Would You Like Guaranteed Income for Life?

*"Peace of mind is the basis of a healthy
body and a healthy mind."*

Dalai Lama

"You're here because you're afraid of outliving your retirement income, right?" Michael asks, not missing a beat.

"Yes!" Susan blurts out and then frowns apologetically at Jason.

Michael nods. "Many Americans are afraid of that, too. People are living longer than ever before, and today, one of the biggest concerns on the minds of many is outliving retirement income. Even if you've saved a substantial amount of money throughout your lifetime, a retirement that lasts for 20 or more years could easily stretch those savings to far beyond what is required — even for just your basic monthly needs.

"Unlike retirees in the past who typically had more than one guaranteed income source to count on, the same may or may not be a reality for you.

"For example, the defined benefit pension plan — also simply referred to as the pension — is quickly disappearing. These plans were offered by many large companies, up until just a couple of decades ago."

"My father had a pension. He never had to worry," Jason said.

Michael nodded. "Many Americans had pensions, and for participants in a pension plan, the employer would promise to pay a set amount of retirement income for life - and because of this, the liability of the pension rested entirely with the employer, not the employee.

"Unfortunately, due in large part to the expense, most employers have done away with defined benefit pension plans over the years and have instead turned to offering defined contribution plans — the most popular of which is the 401(k).

"And we all know how problematic a 401(k) plan can be," Michael says while Jason nods.

"We sure do," Susan says.

How much is enough?

Over the past decade or so, we've been literally deluged with negative news about Wall Street and what's happening with our country's economic and financial situation overall - and rightly so. Job losses, rising prices, and uncertainty - it all can make it difficult to save for the future.

It has been estimated that the stock market crash "erased" nearly $7 trillion of investors' wealth in 2008 alone[39], and many people have not yet fully recovered from that. But even if you have been setting aside a decent amount of money for retirement lately, the still-volatile stock market, combined with historically low interest rates, has provided more than just a slight challenge to ensuring that you will have enough.

What exactly is *enough*?

That depends. You've likely seen ads that tout how you need to reach "your number" or hit your "retirement red zone." But the reality is that what matters the most in retirement is that you have enough *income* to pay for the things that you need and want.

Plus, you'll need to be able to do so for a longer period of time than your grandparents, and maybe even your parents did. That's because our life expectancies have gotten so much longer today than ever before.

In today's economy, it takes strategic planning to ensure that you have the income you need when it comes time to retire. Unfortunately, just simply investing some funds in the market every month won't do the trick. And, having just some income won't do the trick, either.

For example, some people find that when they get to retirement, they have an income "gap" - a difference between the amount that they need and the amount that they actually have coming in. The time to fix that is now, not then.

So, is your retirement plan on track?

"Even if you have some guaranteed income sources," Michael continues, "such as social security, it may not be enough. Over the past 20 years, there has been talk of the Social Security trust fund running dry, and efforts to 'fix' the issue could result in you receiving a lesser amount of income in retirement and/or having to wait longer to receive it.

"One 'solution' already implemented raised Social Security's full retirement age - the age at which you can receive the full amount of your retirement benefits - from 65 to a maximum of 67, depending on the year of your birth."

Social Security Full Retirement Age

Year of Birth	Minimum Retirement Age for Full Benefits
1937 or Before	65
1938	65 + 2 months
1939	65 + 4 months
1940	65 + 6 months
1941	65 + 8 months
1942	65 + 10 months
1943 to 1954	66
1955	66 + 2 months
1956	66 + 4 months
1957	66 + 6 months
1958	66 + 8 months
1959	66 + 10 months
1960 or After	67

Source: Social Security Administration

"Did you know the Social Security Administration (SSA) itself states that this benefit was never meant to be the only source of income for people when they retire?" Michael asks.

Susan and Jason shake their heads.

"According to the SSA," Michael says, "Social Security replaces [only] about 40% of an average wage earner's income after retiring."

"So, if you don't receive income from a defined benefit pension plan, and you are only able to replace about 40% of your income from Social Security - *if this program still exists at the time of your retirement* - then where will the income that you need in retirement come from?

"A strategy that can create safety, with a potential for higher interest based on positive changes in an external index like the S&P500 is something called an indexed annuity, and it's a very popular retirement strategy," Michael says, smiling.

"Let me stop you right there," Jason says, his smile quickly fading. "I know all about annuities, and we aren't interested." He sits back in his chair, crossing his arms in front of his chest.

"Why?" Michael asks. "What have you heard?"

"The fees are high."

"Ah," Michael replies, leaning back. "You're probably thinking of variable annuities. We don't recommend them because of the high fees like you mention. We also think they don't provide enough protection to justify those fees."

"OK..." Jason says, dubious.

"There are several different types of annuities. Some can help ensure that your money is protected in any type of market, and you can count on having guaranteed income for the remainder of your life – regardless of how long you may live."

"I'm very skeptical," Jason says.

"I understand that but hear me out," Michael replies. "The money inside of an annuity is allowed to grow tax-deferred. This means that, unlike your regular investment account(s), you won't have to pay taxes on the gains until the time you withdraw the funds.

"Also, unlike other qualified tax-deferred accounts, such as a 401(k) or IRA, which are subject to IRS contribution guidelines, a non-qualified annuity means it doesn't have a maximum annual contribution limit. This means that you aren't limited to the amount of premium you can pay into an annuity. However, each insurance carrier will have its own maximum limits, and the interest you earn can still get the tax-deferred growth.

"So, if you've already 'maxed out' your employer-sponsored retirement account and/or personal IRA(s), then an annuity can provide you with yet another avenue for obtaining tax-advantaged growth on your money."

"No limits? Really?" Jason asks.

"Yes, really. Some types of annuities will also offer the ability to earn market index-linked growth while at the same time protecting principal in the event of a market downturn. This scenario can allow you to obtain growth without all the risk of the stock market, all while protecting your nest egg.

"And because of an annuity's lifetime payout option, you don't have to worry about income running out - because the annuity will continue making income payments for the remainder of your lifetime, regardless of how long that may be."

"That really sounds wonderful!" Susan says.

"Did you say there are several different types of annuities?" Jason asks.

"Yes, I did. And which one you choose will depend on your specific goals and whether you are already retired and looking for income right now, or you are still in the 'accumulation' stage and will need retirement income in the future."

"First, an annuity can be either immediate or deferred. This refers to when the income payout will begin from the annuity."

Immediate Annuity — With an immediate annuity, the income payout will begin shortly after you purchase the annuity. These annuities are typically purchased with just one lump sum or a single premium. You may also rollover your retirement plan funds such as an IRA or 401(k) into an immediate annuity. The assets that are in an immediate annuity do not continue to accumulate but rather are simply used for the purpose of distributing income.

*If you are already in retirement, you may want to consider an immediate annuity. With just one lump-sum premium payment or rolling over your retirement

account, this type of annuity can generate an ongoing income for you throughout the remainder of your life. Many annuities can also generate guaranteed lifetime income for a second individual, such as your spouse or partner - although the other individual does not have to be related to you.

Deferred Annuity — If you have a deferred annuity, the income payout will begin at some time in the future. Because of that, funds inside a deferred annuity will accumulate on a tax-deferred basis. You can pay your premiums into a deferred annuity via either a single lump sum, or through periodic premium payments over time. The funds inside a deferred annuity are also allowed to grow on a tax-deferred basis. This means that no tax is due on the gain until the time the funds are withdrawn. Because you may be in a lower income tax bracket at retirement, you could realize a nice amount of tax savings.

"Another distinguishing feature about an annuity is whether it is fixed or variable. This can make a difference in the way that the underlying account performs," says Michael, "as well as the guarantees that you have with regard to your principal."

"What are the differences?" Jason asks.

"With a fixed annuity, the offering insurance company will provide you with a fixed amount of interest that is credited to the account on an annual basis. A key benefit to owning a fixed annuity is the safety of principal that it can offer you, as well as the steady and known stream of income in retirement.

"The tradeoff for that, however, is that the return with a fixed annuity will typically be pretty low. This is especially the case lately, as over the past several years, we have been in a very low interest rate environment. Because of this, many people have shied away from fixed annuities due to their lower returns."

"Low returns aren't very exciting," Susan says, frowning.

Michael laughs, "No, they aren't. However, if you want potentially higher returns, a variable annuity will allow you to participate in equity vehicles, such as mutual funds, that are set up in 'sub-accounts.' Because of this, the value of a variable annuity's account has the opportunity to grow substantially over time.

"However, due to their market exposure, and also because variable annuities do not protect consumers against market losses, these types of annuities can be considered more risky than fixed annuities. A variable annuity may provide you with the ability for growth, but that return could disappear the next time there is a market 'correction' or even a slight downturn, depending on the underlying equities in the annuity's sub-accounts."

"Those are also the annuities with the high fees, right?" Jason asks.

"Yes," Michael replies, nodding his head. "High fees are associated with variable annuities, which, as I mentioned, we don't recommend.

"There is one more type of annuity to mention: fixed index annuities. It's a newer generation of fixed annuity that has its return linked to the performance of an underlying market index, such as the S&P 500. With this type of annuity, when the index performs well over a given period, the value of the account has the opportunity to rise, sometimes fairly significantly.

"However, if the index performs poorly over a certain period of time, unlike with a variable annuity, your principal is protected, and you don't lose any principal during that period. However, some index annuities do have annual fees or penalties for taking money out before 59 ½, in addition to a surrender charge for taking money out early."

"That sounds too good to be true!" Susan says, beaming.

"Yes, I hear that a lot," Michael says, laughing. "A fixed index annuity can essentially provide you with the ability to obtain growth, while at the same time, protecting funds from market downturns."

Fixed Index Annuities Additional Benefits*

- Turn the income stream "on" or "off"
- Withdraw a portion of the annuity's value without penalty

- Retain access to the annuity's initial value
- Provide income for two individuals.

*Annuity benefits vary by state and may not be available in all states.

"How does all of this work?" Jason asks.

"Annuities are contracts between an individual and an insurance company, and in return for either a lump-sum premium or periodic premium payments into the annuity, they guarantee a stream of income to the person named on the annuity*."

Michael continues, "Annuities are also often used as accumulation vehicles for retirement savings. The money grows tax-deferred, like we talked about, which is the case regardless of whether your annuity is fixed or variable.

"In most cases, you will be allowed to withdraw up to 10% of your total contract value each year, without penalty from your annuity. This means that if you have some type of an emergency and you absolutely need the funds, you can retrieve them from your account.

"One thing I always make sure I mention to my clients is that annuities have a surrender period or a certain number of

---

* *The person on whom the annuity's income stream is based is referred to as the annuitant - and even though the annuitant is oftentimes also the owner of the annuity, they do not necessarily have to be.*

years where you will be penalized if you withdraw more than the penalty-free withdrawal amount of your funds from the annuity."

"That means we should consider an annuity as a long-term strategy?" Susan asks.

"That's exactly right," Michael replies.

Highly Attractive Fixed Index Annuity Features

Fixed Rate of Return - Just as with other fixed annuities, a fixed index annuity offers a guaranteed minimum rate of return on your money.

Additional Growth Potential - Because the funds inside of a fixed index annuity are also tied in part to the performance of an underlying market index, they have the potential to return more than their guaranteed minimum. Fixed index annuities may credit interest in different ways, depending on the specific annuity. For example, some fixed index annuities use a monthly average, while others use a method referred to as an annual point-to-point. Still others use a monthly sum method of crediting interest. Growth is typically "capped" at a certain amount - but in return, the principal is also shielded from market downturns.

Protection of Principal - If the underlying index performs poorly during a given time period, the principal is protected, so there will be no loss in the account.

Annual Reset – Annual Reset Value compares of the underlying index's year-end value to the start of the following year. This will determine the amount of interest that you will be credited based upon the performance of the index and the annuity contract's terms. Depending on the insurance company, these are typically reset every one to two years.

Legacy Benefits - Legacy benefits can often be added, sometimes for a charge, as an additional rider to the fixed index annuity. Here, you can protect your annuity's principal if you have spent into your annuity funds. With this benefit, the principal can pass on in full to your beneficiary.

Nursing Home/Long-term Care Rider - Many index annuities today will also offer long-term care or nursing home riders that allow additional liquidity if you should require certain types of care. This means that you may be able to access a certain amount of the annuity's funds without penalty if you are required to move to a nursing home facility for a certain amount of time.

Additional Income Guarantees - While all annuities can provide a stream of income, fixed index annuities may offer you the ability to add an income rider, sometimes for a charge, that allows additional income guarantees. (These are discussed in more detail later in this guide).

* Not all of these features and riders are available with all fixed index annuities or in all states.

"Can we go back to 'guaranteed income for life?' I still don't understand how that works exactly," says Jason.

"Certainly. One of the most appealing features of an annuity is the fact that it can alleviate the concerns you may have about running out of retirement income before you run out of time."

"Depending on your specific circumstances, you may be able to structure the income payout stream for a certain number of years, the remainder of your lifetime only, or even the remainder of your and someone else's lifetime."

Income Payment Options (Typically) Allowed on Annuities

Life Only - The life only option will provide you with income payments from your annuity for the remainder of your lifetime - no matter how long that may be. Income payments will end at your death. No payments will be made to your beneficiary.

Joint and Survivor - The joint and survivor income payout option is often used by couples who want to ensure that both spouses and partners will receive income for the remainder of their lifetimes. In this case, the annuity will continue paying out until both of the individuals have passed away. In some instances, the dollar amount may be reduced upon the death of the first person. In other cases, it may remain the same.

Period Certain - If you choose the period certain option, the annuity will pay out a regular recurring payment for a certain number of years - no matter how long you live. This means that after the number of years has ended, the annuity will stop paying out income. Conversely, if you pass away early, the annuity will continue to make payments to a named beneficiary until the end of the stated time period.

Life with Period Certain - The life with period certain option is essentially a combination of the period certain option with the life only option. This is because the annuity will pay out income for the rest of your lifetime. However, if you pass away within a short period of time, the annuity will keep paying out income for a set amount of time, or "period certain," to a named beneficiary.

"I think we can agree that everyone's retirement goals are different, right?"

"Yes, definitely," Jason and Susan both say, almost in unison.

"Fixed index annuities with income riders can be a great way to give yourself more control over how and when you receive retirement income, in addition to providing you with a guaranteed income for life.

"In the past, when you were ready to convert an annuity over to an income stream, annuitize the contract, for example, you would essentially lose control of the money. This was in exchange for your guarantee of receiving your ongoing income payments from the annuity. In some cases, if you passed away - even if death occurred soon after the income payments started - the insurance company would retain the remainder of your premiums.

"While there are still some annuities like this available in the market, today there are also a whole new array of options available to choose from, options that provide you and your loved ones with much better alternatives. One of these options is the guaranteed income rider."

"What's that?" asks Jason.

"An income rider can essentially offer you additional income guarantees with your annuity. As an example, an income rider can be added where interest is paid at a variable rate with no principal fluctuations.

"In this case, a separate account is actually created from your base annuity account. This isn't a cash account, but simply an account from which to base your future income. The amount of income is then determined by the value in the income account and the growth credited to your account over time. This can help to provide you with a set return as well as a predictable income stream in the future.

"In some cases, you are also able to turn 'on' income payments when you want them and turn them 'off' when they are not needed. By doing so, you can manage your retirement cash flow and tax liability when not receiving annuity income.

"Then, depending on how long you leave your income 'off,' it is possible that the amount of your income payment could increase by the time that you turn it on again in the future."

Annuity Income Rider Benefits*

- Retain access to the initial purchase value of the annuity.
- Turn the annuity's income stream on or off as you desire.
- Withdraw a portion of the annuity's value each year without penalty.

*Benefits may not be available in all states and may carry additional fees

---

"I don't know," says Jason, wrinkling his brow. "I'm still skeptical. My entire life, I've been told annuities are a scam and that only the insurance companies win out."

Myth #1: People will lose their money to the insurance company when they die.

"That's a common misconception," Michael says, nodding his head. "While there are still some annuities that are set up this way, there are other ways in which you can ensure that you do not lose your premiums to the insurance company."

"For example, one way to do so is to opt for the return of premium rider or buy an annuity with a Death Benefit. In these cases, you can name a beneficiary who will receive back the premium that you paid into the annuity contract."

"OK, so I can ensure that any excess cash goes to one of my beneficiaries?" Jason asks.

"Yes, that's correct."

"I just thought of something," says Susan. "My sister Joanie told me that annuities are only for people who don't already have a retirement account."

Myth #2: If you already have a retirement account, you do not need an annuity.

"How much income are you guaranteed to get from your other retirement account?" Michael asks.

"Guaranteed? I don't know. I don't think any of it is *guaranteed*," Susan replies.

"Right," Michael responds, leaning forward, "a 401(k) is a retirement account. Although you may be saving funds in a tax-deferred account such as a 401(k) or an IRA, as we now know, these accounts don't guarantee a lifetime income in retirement like an annuity can. Therefore, an annuity should still be a consideration, especially as you inch closer to retirement."

"But how do we know returns from annuities really exist? How do we know we'll actually get good returns?" Jason asks.

Myth #3: Hypothetical returns aren't realistic.

"I understand your concern," Michael says, "because I was concerned about that, too. But the returns that are produced by annuities are, in fact, real. And, when it comes to the fixed index annuity, these vehicles have actually produced some very nice returns ever since the very first one was purchased in February 1995.[40]

"In fact, over a 12-year period, the average return range of these fixed index annuities actually outperformed the S&P 500 in most years. Keeping in mind that past performance does not equate to future performance."

Michael slides a chart across the table toward Jason and Susan.

Annualized Five-Year Returns

Period	S&P 500	FIA Ave. Return	No. of FIAs	Return Range
1997-2002	9.39%	9.19%	5	7.80% to 12.16%
1998-2003	-0.42%	5.46%	13	3.00% to 7.97%
1999-2004	-2.77%	4.69%	8	3.00% to 6.63%
2000-2005	-3.08%	4.33%	28	0.85% to 8.66%
2001-2006	5.11%	4.36%	13	1.91% to 6.55%
2002-2007	13.37%	6.12%	23	3.00% to 8.39%
2003-2008	3.18%	6.05%	19	3.00% to 7.80%
2004-2009	-1.05%	4.19%	27	2.25% to 6.83%

Source: Wharton Financial Institution Center

After they have a chance to read the chart, Michael continues speaking.

"Regardless of how old you currently are, or where you currently have your savings, having an annuity can be a great way to diversify your overall retirement portfolio and put you on your way to ensuring that you will have guaranteed income for life in the future."

"This really is making a lot of sense," Susan says before taking a sip from a glass of water on the table.

"For some people, especially people worried about running out of money in retirement, annuities are a great solution." Michael smiles. "But before we talk about the features you should look for when building the annuity that's right for you, I want to address the fees. I know it's something you're both concerned about."

"Yes, please," says Susan.

"That would be great," Jason says.

Myth #4: Annuities charge high fees.

"Like we've talked about, the fees are the highest with variable annuities, which we don't recommend, but like most other types of financial products, there can be fees that are charged when you buy an annuity.

"For example, if you choose an optional rider such as the income rider I mentioned earlier, then you may be charged an additional amount in exchange for these benefits.

There are annuities that don't charge a fee; however, they will still have a surrender charge. Some annuities even give you bonuses when you get started. In comparison to investments such as mutual funds, the fees that you are charged for your annuity are often minimal - especially as a fixed index annuity can offer you guarantees when it comes to the protection of principal from market volatility as well as ongoing lifetime income in retirement."

Michael looked at Jason and Susan from across the table.

"How does all that sound?"

"It sounds good, Michael," Jason says, nodding his head. "I understand that the growth may not be out of this world, but for peace of mind, it sounds worth it."

"Yes, and that chart you showed us was really helpful," Susan adds.

"Great," says Michael, smiling. "Are you two ready to talk features?"

"Yes!" They both say.

"I think we all can agree that the income you have in retirement can make a big difference in your lifestyle, and ultimately in your life. That's why planning for that income *now* is so important."

Jason and Susan nod their heads energetically.

"When you're ready to take the next step and move forward with the purchase of an annuity, it is important to ensure that you have the right annuity for you because not all annuities are the same. This is especially the case when it comes to fixed index annuity vehicles."

"Based on your individual needs, there are several factors you should consider. The first is the annuity's minimum guaranteed value return. You need to know the percentage return you're going to receive from the annuity. The annuity will create a rate of interest to a percentage of the premium.

"You also need to know which index (or indexes) the annuity will be tracking and the crediting method that will be used so you can monitor changes.

"The surrender charge on the annuity needs to be considered, as well as the contractual details of that income rider. Finally, before signing on the dotted line, you want to make sure the insurance company offering the annuity is financially strong and stable."

Fixed Index Annuity - Key Factors

Minimum Guaranteed Value Return - One criteria important to know is the annuity's guaranteed minimum value return (such as 2%, 3%, etc.). The annuity will create a rate of interest to a percentage of the premium.

Index(es) Tracked - You will also want to know which index (or indexes, if there is more than one) the annuity will be tracking. Often, an insurance company will allow the annuity holder to choose from several different options, such as the S&P 500, NASDAQ and the like.

Crediting Method - Knowing the crediting method used will help you know how the changes in the index will be tracked.

Surrender Charge - Another key factor to note is the surrender charge on the annuity. Here, you will want to know the percentage as well as how many years the annuity will impose a surrender charge.

Guaranteed Income Rider Contractual Details

and Any Costs or Charges - If you are planning to take income later on, you will also want to inquire about the contractual details of the guaranteed income rider.

Strength of the Offering Insurer - It is also important to be sure that the insurance company you're purchasing the annuity through is strong and stable from a financial standpoint and that it has a good reputation for paying out its policyholder claims. You can typically find out information about insurance companies on your state's Department of Insurance website.

"There sure is a lot to consider," Jason says, looking over-whelmed.

"Yes, there is," says Susan, equally frazzled.

"Having a qualified professional on your side, who is well versed in fixed index annuities, can be extremely helpful when you are considering the purchase of a fixed index annuity. Working with a financial professional allows you to have all of your questions answered as you go through the process, so you know exactly how your annuity will work - and how it will work for *you*."

"I definitely have a lot of questions," Susan says.

Michael nods his head. "While fixed index annuities offer many great benefits, it is important to note that these products are not all exactly the same - and because of that, it is best to work with an annuity professional who can help you in determining which one may be the most suitable for you, based on your specific needs and goals.

"Regardless of what happens with the stock market, interest rates, or even the economy overall, when you own a fixed indexed annuity, you will have greater assurance that you will have retirement income that lasts as long as you do - guaranteed."

Jason looks at Susan, who nods. Then, he excitedly asks, "How do we get started?"

Chapter 9:

FINANCE YOURSELF TO WEALTH

"Those who understand interest earn it, those who don't, pay it."
—ALBERT EINSTEIN

"Before you decide on an annuity, let me share the most popular strategy used to defeat all of the enemies of wealth we discussed today. It provides 6 important benefits: First, you will not lose money in the stock market because your money is not in the stock market. Although you could have fees and surrender charges. Second, during good years you can grow your money based in part on the performance of the underlying index and crediting method used to potentially outpace inflation.

"Third, experts call this the biggest benefit left in the tax code because your money grows tax-deferred, and you can access it tax-preferred. Fourth, it can provide a supplemental retirement cash flow that could last until age 100 if structured and funded correctly. Fifth, you can use your money to become your own source of financing. Sixth, it is a self-completing insurance policy, so if you pass away before you can save enough for your family to live on, the insurance benefit will provide the money needed."

"In very simple terms," Michael explains, "the IUL, short for Indexed Universal Life, is a customized cash value life insurance policy. In the next few minutes, I'm going to show you how it not only provides protection but can be a powerful wealth accumulation tool."

(We are spending time here because this is the foundation.)

"Oh, no!" Susan cries. "Hold on! I've heard both Suze Orman and Dave Ramsey say that it's a bad idea to buy cash value life insurance!"

"Yeah," Jason chimes in. "My buddy who's a CPA says cash value life insurance is the wrong way to go. Lots of the financial pieces I've studied paint a poor picture of cash value life insurance, too. They say it's just too expensive."

"I'm going to debunk those myths for you in just a few minutes," Michael says, "and you're going to clearly see how cash value life insurance—*if* it's structured and funded properly— can be a very solid alternative solution for building wealth."

"Better than term insurance?" Jason asks.

"It's in a different league than term insurance," Michael says.

"Term insurance is important for one reason; to provide for your family in the event of an untimely death. It's a bit like renting, really. You rent the insurance for a set period of years, and after that term of 10 or 20 years is up, your insurance is gone, or you have to pay more for a similar amount of insurance, because you are that much older. There's usually no equity in term policies. However, if you do happen to die during those years, your beneficiaries receive the death benefit from your policy."

Michael continues, "We, as Americans, spend more money insuring our cars than we do our lives. In fact, we actually do things in reverse: we focus on protecting the golden eggs—cars, homes, and other possessions—instead of protecting the goose that lays those golden eggs."

"I have to admit I'm guilty of that," Jason murmurs. "Pretty much all I've got is my little policy through work—a term policy—but, man, I sure shell it out on insurance for the cars and the house." Michael nods in understanding.

"Using cash value insurance like an IUL can provide death benefit protection like term, along with a protected place for your money. It's sometimes referred to as *permanent* life insurance. And it's just what its name implies, too: it covers you until you die as long as you keep the policy in force. While we've all watched the stock market rise and fall, with banks and companies failing, the insurance industry has stayed solid. Did you know that during the Great Depression, while the banks and Wall Street crashed, the insurance industry not only maintained its strength but kept its promises? During the Great Depression, clearly, the greatest period of economic stress to date in the nation's history, policyholder cash values in life insurance companies were unaffected. Contrast that with the estimated 9,000-10,000 banks that failed during that time[26] and again in 2010, when over 143 banks failed.[27]"

"Wow, I had no idea," Jason says.

"I like to look at history," Michael explains. "From the early 1930s until about 1980, life insurance companies—not Wall Street—were the dominant architects, builders, and custodians of the nation's savings and retirement systems.[28]

Jason splits the air with a low whistle. "I'm surprised—I really am. I didn't know any of that. But here's my question: my current policy, as I said, is term life. I've looked at prices, and, quite frankly, term is less money each month."

"Well, remember the reason we're here—it's not just to talk insurance. It's to show you how you could grow wealth without risking your money in the stock market," Michael explains. "A term life policy usually doesn't provide any benefits to you while you're living. A permanent cash value life policy provides quite a few significant benefits to you while you're still alive.

A term policy typically doesn't build cash value; whereas a permanent cash value life policy is designed to do exactly that when it is structured and funded properly."

"So why isn't everybody doing this," Susan asks. "If cash value is so good, why haven't I heard more about it?"

"That's a very good question," Michael says. "As good as cash value insurance is, it's important to realize that all cash value policies don't work the same way. The criticisms targeted at permanent insurance often revolve around the fact that agents make large commissions on traditional policies. Also, too much of your money or yearly premiums buy insurance instead of building cash value.

"For the IUL, we've chosen companies that will allow you to max-fund above the cost of insurance, so long as the policy is not a Modified Endowment Contract (MEC). Your premium payments are used to pay the cost of insurance, and anything above those costs is allocated to an indexed account that receives interest credit based on the performance of the underlying index and the crediting method used, which is then added to build the cash value side of the policy. Typically, this means that you can put as much money as possible toward your cash value and as little as possible toward the actual insurance costs as long as you stay within the MEC limits.

"The vast majority of financial professionals and insurance agents don't know how to do this properly to maximize the cash value growth.

They've never been trained. You certainly don't get this advanced training when you study for your license! That's why it is good to work with an insurance professional or an independent agent whose specialty is to maximize your cash growth, not your insurance costs.

Crash Proof Wealth

Going this route typically cuts an agent's commission about in half, but an insurance professional will gladly do it because it's better for their clients. However, many agents don't see it this way,

they'd rather double up the commission at the cost of the client...
that is *not* the kind of agent you would want to do business with if
you are trying to build an alternate strategy.

"The secret is not only working with an agent who understands
how to structure the policy correctly, but also in working with
companies who support the concept," Michael explains. "How
does this change your view of life insurance?"

"Again, let's step back a moment from the story and review
the key ingredients for building an IUL to accomplish what we
have talked about. Here are a few of the most important pieces:

1. You want an insurance company with a long history of
   success and financial stability, companies that have been
   in business for over 100 years.

2. You need an agent who has been trained to structure a
   policy for maximum cash value growth and minimum
   death benefit, all without hurting your tax advantages.

3. You need a company that will allow you to maximize
   cash value growth while minimizing your insurance
   costs. This is critical!

4. When you take a loan, your money can continue to grow
   as though you've never borrowed against your policy.

The 6 Great Crash Proof Wealth Strategies

Let's say you buy the finest-quality chocolate bar available (representing term life insurance). You love chocolate and would like nothing more than to sink your teeth into that bar, but the people from whom you bought it say you can't do that. By law, you have to put it away. You can't touch it. It won't go to waste, though. As soon as you die, your heirs get to savor that chocolate bar on the way home from your funeral.

Who wants to buy a chocolate bar they can't even enjoy? You sure wouldn't want to pay much for it, would you? That's why term life is so popular: it costs less. In fact, it's the smallest amount of money you can pay in premiums and still provide a death benefit for your beneficiaries. But take a look at the reason it costs so much less—it's only in effect for a specified length of time, and it provides benefits only to your beneficiaries. There's no benefit to you.

Okay, back to the chocolate bar metaphor. Now, say you buy the finest-quality chocolate bar available (representing cash value life insurance). This time, though, you're able to savor that chocolate bar while you're still alive. In fact, your chocolate bar keeps getting bigger and bigger—so, not only do you get to *keep* enjoying it, but when you die, your beneficiaries will have even more chocolate to enjoy together. And while they're enjoying the smooth sweetness, they'll do so with the satisfaction of knowing you enjoyed it, too.

"Basically, here's what happens," Michael explains. "You buy a properly structured cash value life policy that you agree to pay into each month. Your money is not invested in the market. Instead, your premium payments are used to pay the cost of insurance, and anything above those costs is allocated to an indexed account that receives interest credits based on the performance of the underlying index.

Even if you borrow from it, and even when you take tax-advantaged cash flow from it during retirement, you've got an alternate financial product that can provide cash flow for you in retirement as long as you pay your premiums, one that is structured and funded properly.

Your principal is protected from market downturns, so you won't lose it during market swings. You will still have costs and expenses, and some years you might not make a return, but your policy will not receive a negative crediting either. And you get what we call *living benefits* from an IUL."

There are actually several other wealth accumulation options you can use depending on your situation and your goals. Income for Life options can guarantee that you never outlive your money. This can be a great peace of mind for folks going into retirement. There are also what we call "supercharged" IULs that allow you to benefit from the ups of market growth without losses due to market volatility. This is really exciting and will be covered in a subsequent chapter.

From here on, when we—and Michael—talk about cash value insurance, we're talking about the kind of IUL that provides these powerful benefits to you. Just about anyone can use it (you don't need to be educated or experienced), and it works on autopilot (you don't have to watch the market, reassess stocks based on performance or worry about tax consequences as long as it's structured and funded properly and you can qualify for the insurance). And while it requires a bit of patience, and depending on what you are trying to accomplish, it can work whether you have thousands or just a few hundred to set aside each month.

Keep in mind, like with anything, the shorter your time horizon, the more you may have to put in, or be open to the possibility of adjusting your time horizon. Now, let's get back to the story.

"So far, it's sounding pretty good," says Susan, "but what do you mean by *living benefits?*"

"I've already mentioned a few," Michael responds. "The IUL gives you protection that is guaranteed by the insurance company that your principal is immune from whatever the stock market is doing. You will still have costs and expenses even in years you may not receive an interest credit; however your policy will not receive negative crediting because of a market downturn. Another benefit is taxes. The IRA expert Ed Slott says, "Life insurance is the single biggest benefit to the IRS tax code."[29] You save taxes on the growth of your principal, you can access the cash value without paying taxes, and when the death benefit is paid out to your beneficiaries, it comes to them income tax-free in most cases because you paid taxes on the money before you put it into your policy.

And remember that one of the risks of 401(k) plans and mutual funds is the risk that the government could change the rules midstream due to the latest political agenda or bureaucratic whim," Michael says. "With an IUL, your policy is a private contract between you and the insurance company."

"Of course, one of the greatest living benefits is your ability to reduce or totally stop paying interest to banks and Finance Yourself to Wealth™," Michael explains.

"How does that work?" Jason asks.

"We'll use a car for an example. Let's say you want to buy a $20,000 car. You can get a loan from a bank or car financing company, or in your case, use your IUL to finance the car.

With traditional car financing, you might finance the car for five years or so. In the end, you have a car paid off, and you've lost all the interest and principal to the finance company.

When you Finance Yourself to Wealth,™ you borrow against your IUL policy and pay for the car in cash. (Often, paying cash can save you money on the purchase price by itself.) Then you make payments back to your policy. This is where it gets exciting— after the five years, you've got your car paid off, but you also have the $20,000 back into your IUL!

Plus, you can pay additional interest with your payments, and the extra money will increase your cash value. This is why we call it Financing Yourself to Wealth™. Because each time you take out a loan and pay it back with extra interest, it can increase your cash value."

"That sounds interesting," Susan says.

"With a cash value insurance policy." Michael continues, "You have access to the cash value in your policy, and you can't be turned down for a loan. If you need to borrow the cash value from your policy, just say the word. No credit check, no tax returns, no qualifying hassle. And no one's going to raise your interest rate if you're late on a payment. In fact, *you* determine the repayment timetable, and *you* decide how often and for how long you want to make payments."

"This almost sounds too good to be true," Jason says.

"It gets even better," Michael responds. "Remember when we talked about how one of the enemies of wealth is interest? When you use your IUL to finance your purchases, your money continues to grow, as though you never touched a dime. When you pay the loan back, you recoup the cost of that purchase back into your policy rather than making payments to someone else. As a result, you can enjoy some of the things you'd like without destroying your nest egg."

By this time, Jason and Susan are both wide-eyed. "There's got to be a hitch," Susan says, "and I can think of a big one. I'm not sure we'd even qualify for insurance right now. I just had some really serious health problems."

"If you're too old or have health issues that might make you uninsurable, you're not out of luck," Michael explains. "You can buy a policy on a child, spouse, or grandchild who does qualify to be insured. You own the policy, and you still control it, so you decide what happens to the money. So, let's assume you can qualify. If your policy is structured properly, your policy is permanent. That means as long as you keep it in force, it will be with you forever. This is extremely important when it comes to taxes. Life insurance is one of the best estate tax planning vehicles there is because it gets paid to your estate income tax-free.

Michael adds, "That's another one of the great benefits: your life is insured. The average man in this country has an economic value of more than one million dollars. If you die, especially if you die early, your family could suffer a significant economic loss on top of the emotional sorrow of losing you. The death benefit of life insurance provides financially for those you leave behind. In fact, as long as it's in force, your policy will generally pay out a lump-sum income-tax-free death benefit that's far larger than the total premiums."

"Now, keep in mind, as we're referencing Financing Yourself to Wealth™, we're talking about policy loans, not withdrawals. Withdrawals are when you permanently take the money out of the policy. We use loans because your money continues to grow if you are using an indexed or variable participating loan, even while you are using it. Then, as you pay it back, it is there for you to use again and again."

"So, what happens if we can't pay the loans back?" asks Susan.

"The idea is to be able to structure the loans so they can be paid back, similar to a regular car loan. If for some reason, you can't make payments for a while, it's not a huge deal. No one will be knocking on your door to collect. You simply resume paying when you can. If you pass away before you pay the loan back, then the loan and the interest on the loan will be subtracted from the death benefit, and what is left over will be paid out to the beneficiaries. However, you definitely want to pay the loans back if you are using them for Financing Yourself to Wealth™."

"But what happens if we can't for some reason?" Susan asks.

"You will want to continue to pay interest on the loan because the loan interest will accrue, and ultimately the policy could lapse and cancel.[30] Just like gardening—if you stop watering a plant, it stops growing. We want to keep nurturing the IUL so it continues to grow. This goes back to making sure your policy is properly structured and funded. Then once you hit your retirement years, we have conservatively structured your policy so that you have enough cash value that the interest from the index is paying for the cost of insurance and more, and you never have to pay more premiums into it. It can then be there to provide tax advantaged retirement cash flow."

"But," Michael says. "Here's the real beauty of a loan from your policy: *you* structure the repayment schedule. *You* determine how much you can pay and how often you want to pay.

"Makes sense, but is there a limit to how much we can put in?" Jason asks.

"Yes," Michael says. "We want to make sure that your policy doesn't become a Modified Endowment Contract (MEC). In order to enjoy the maximum tax benefits of your IUL, you want to keep the policy within the MEC limit.

The IRS has set up guidelines that dictate how much cash value you can put into a policy compared to the insurance amount. If you exceed their limits, meaning you put in too much cash, it could have negative tax implications—essentially ruining one of the major benefits of getting an IUL. As an insurance professional, I prefer to structure the policy to stay under the MEC limit in order to enjoy maximum tax advantages.

"Yeah," Jason replies, "I can see why we want to work with someone who's been trained to do this properly. I'd hate to lose out on tax savings just because of an untrained agent."

"If this is so great," Susan chimes in, "why haven't I heard anything about it? Is it because it's new?"

"Absolutely not," Michael answers. "In fact, Americans have been using permanent life insurance policies for over 100 years. Large companies, business people, and average citizens protect their capital by buying cash value life insurance policies on their employees and then using them as strong foundations. One reason why you might not have heard about it is that gurus, bankers, and Wall Street have no interest in promoting these policies because they often want you to invest in the market."

"Okay," Jason nods. "So how do we get started?"

"The bottom line is this," Michael explains. "You can start by funding an IUL, a special type of cash value insurance life policy. Then, instead of borrowing from a bank, you borrow from your policy. You simply use a different way to pay for things—a method that lets you recoup the cost of large purchases instead of letting that money go into a lender's pocket. And all the while you're growing a tidy nest egg, one you can predict and, even better, one you can count on."

"That *sounds* good," Susan agrees, "but I'm not sure I understand. Why not just put my money in an interest-bearing savings account and then use that money to buy the things I want? Wouldn't I actually come out ahead in the long run?"

"First," Michael replies, "how much does your money grow in a bank account while you aren't using it for something else?

1.5 - 2%, if you are lucky? If you invest in a bond or CD, the percentage of growth will be a little higher. Now consider this: with an IUL, not only can your money grow between a floor of zero and a cap, but if you structure and fund it right—and as an insurance professional, I know how to do it right—you could also receive growth when the market goes up, without risking your money in the market."

"But here's the part of the answer that's really convincing," Michael continues. "Let's say you deposit your money in a bank account and then withdraw the $20,000 we talked about to pay cash for a car. Does the bank continue to pay you interest on the money you withdrew? Of course not. But guess what? Your IUL policy *does*. That's the amazing thing about an IUL. People really think it is too good to be true, yet it is true, and it can be a great financial tool for those who take advantage of it."

"I've got to admit I'm pretty stunned by all this."

Jason says, "I just went through a pretty big hassle with the 401(k) deal—are there rules here? I mean, what kinds of things can I borrow money for?"

"You can borrow from your account for anything you want," Michael answers. "You can run many of your large purchases through it—cars, vacations, business expenses, home improvement, and even real estate purchases. It's your money, and no one's going to tell you what you can do with it."

"So, it's like our own source of financing," Susan says. "But we set the terms and have more control over it."

"Exactly," says Michael. "In the end, what your IUL policy really can give you is a solid foundation. A foundation for your overall financial plan that you can count on without risking your principal, worrying about what the market is doing, and getting access to your money if something comes up. It's a predictable and protected way to put away your money. Following this approach could ultimately create millions of dollars in wealth for you and your family while allowing you to reduce the amount of interest you are paying to banks, credit cards, or other financial institutions."

The relief on Jason's face is obvious. "After what we've been through, this would really allow me to sleep well at night," he says.

"Absolutely." Michael responds. "You don't even have to wait until you retire. You get to enjoy the benefits now. For example, we can structure and fund the IUL and if you want to take a family vacation next year, just get started now. When the time comes, you pull out a couple thousand dollars and go. Then pay the loan back, and you recoup the cost of that vacation. Then, it's there for you when you need it next time."

"So, we can use it for the kitchen remodel we're thinking of doing too, huh?" says Susan.

"Absolutely," Michael replies. "Home improvement, college, cars, even investing in a business or real estate—whatever you want. Then when you're ready to retire, you can take loans without having to pay taxes on that money as long as it is structured and funded properly."

"I'm pretty much sold," Jason says, and Susan nods. "But as you can imagine, we don't have a lot of cash on hand right now. How much do we have to put in to get started?"

"The cost to you is only the amount you want to pay in premiums," Michael says. "There are several different ways to get started. Some folks redirect savings from current income, some move part of their savings sitting in the bank over; in fact, there are many different ways to find money to fund an IUL. Remember, you will want to structure the IUL so that your premium payments are used to pay the cost of insurance, and anything above those costs is allocated to an indexed account that receives interest credits."

"But we have to make monthly premium payments, right?" asks Susan.

"Not necessarily," says Michael. "It's very flexible. You could pay all up front, pay yearly, or even set up what I call an "automatic wealth-building machine." This would automatically transfer money from your bank account and pay your premiums each month without you worrying about it. But I imagine the real question you were trying to ask is how you're going to come up with the extra money. That's something specific I want to talk over with you. There are quite a few places I can help you find money to fund your policy. I'm confident that you can easily— and probably painlessly—divert money from other sources to build your cash value without changing your lifestyle. Let's start with the most obvious: how much money do you get back on tax returns each year?"

Jason says, "About $4,000 - $5,000."

"Okay, so that's about $400 extra dollars every month you are sending to the IRS for no reason. Is there a reason you like to let Uncle Sam use your money for 12 months without paying you a dime of interest on it?"

"Well, when you put it like that, no, I guess it's not a good idea, is it? I just don't want to have to pay extra when the tax time comes around," Jason finishes.

"I understand. It's easy to set your deductions so that you still get a small refund while allowing most of your money to stay with you to use throughout the year. If you add up the $4,000 - $5,000 for the next 15-20 years of your working life, that could be an extra $100,000 you could add to your cash value."

"Well, sheesh," Susan breaks in, "We should do that immediately!"

"We can build a policy that works for you. One client bought cash value policies on each of his boys when they were very young. At the time, his intention was to accumulate some cash but to also provide them with death benefit coverage when they became adults and responsible for their individual families. As it turns out, one is now married with one daughter. He has cash value that can be used for his daughter's college expenses, braces, family vacations, or new cars. The young son, who is still single, has cash value to continue his college degree, replace his vehicle when the time comes, or make a down payment on a home."

"So, we could set these up for our kids as well?" Susan asks.

"Yes. In fact, once you get your own IUL in place, many people end up with multiple policies in the family. Kids can use them for college funding options or to pay for their first car or house." Michael replies.

"So, once we get started, can we start using the money right away, or do we have to wait?" Jason asks.

"It will depend on how we structure and fund the policy. Remember, your premium payments are used to pay the cost of insurance, and anything above those costs is allocated to an index account. You will have policy fees and expenses that you will need to consider as well. Optimally it's best to wait and allow the policy to accumulate some cash value and gain some interest. The risk with borrowing too soon from your policy is your loan will most likely be a fixed loan and not participate in the index. I mentioned that previously. The best thing to do is talk about how much you want to put in the IUL, how much your remodeling project will cost, and then run some numbers to see the earliest time you can access your cash value for this project. Once you are approved for the IUL and are ready to access your cash value, you can usually access your cash value within a couple of weeks. Also, as I mentioned earlier, you will want to pay back your loan so that you can fund future projects and supplement future financial needs..."

"It's important to realize that an IUL is not a get-rich-quick scheme," emphasizes Michael. "It's a long-term approach to put you on the path to becoming wealthy outside Wall Street. It requires diligence and patience."

"You keep talking about becoming a millionaire. If, using your approach, we were able to cut back on some of the areas where we are currently wasting money, change my withholdings so that I keep more of my tax money throughout the year, and redirect my $550 per month 401(k) contributions over...that's... about $400 per month on taxes, $550 on our 401(k) and we're wasting another $50 per month right now on extra landline phone we don't use...

So how much could we have if we put about $1000 per month into a policy?" Jason asks.

"Good question, this is the beauty of the IUL— by

structuring and funding your IUL properly, it allows us to put money away and know, with relative certainty, how much is going to be there for you when you need it."

Susan chimes in. "Yeah, I'm really tired of opening our 401(k) statement and seeing it go down, down, down!"

"Usually, an IUL performs best the longer you let it grow and compound. When do you think you will want to start taking money out?" Michael asks.

"Well, let's say age 65," Jason replies.

After crunching a few numbers, Michael says, "Assuming that you get average growth of 7% using the indexing strategy (we'll cover this in a second) at the age of 65 you could have right around $643,000 with a death benefit of approximately $929,000 that could go to your spouse or children. But here's the real exciting part...are you ready?[31]"

"Yeah, what have you got?"

"Using these projections, at age 65, you could have an annual cash flow that you access from your cash value without a taxable event, of $86,000 until age 100."

"$86,000 per year...that I get without a taxable event? Wow, that's amazing...especially considering it's not going to get wiped out in a market downturn, and we know we can count on it being protected," Susan says.

"$86,000 per year for 35 years is like 3 million dollars! How is that possible?" Jason says.

"Remember that when you take a variable loan you borrow against your policy, the cash value continues to grow as if it's never been touched. It's also important to remember these projections are made using the insurance company's actuarial projections. They use data from the past 25 years...but they aren't guaranteed. There's a chance it could be less than that."

Susan jumps in, "I appreciate you saying that I hate to be sold a bill of goods only to be disappointed. Even if it's half that amount, having about $43,000 per year to live on until age 100 is pretty fantastic. Plus, that money isn't at risk in the market."

"$1000 might be pushing it for us right now. What would happen if we only did say $500 per month?" Susan asks.

"No problem," Michael says, "With $500 per month, you're still potentially looking at $43,000 every year until age 100. The reason you don't pay tax on this money is that you are taking a loan and borrowing against the policy, not withdrawing the money out of the policy.

Of course, this is the way it works under current IRS tax laws."

"Keep in mind," continues Michael, "these policies work with compound interest. Meaning the more money you put into your policy, the faster your policy grows. Why wouldn't you want to put as much money as possible into a policy that only gets better the more you put in? With traditional financial tools like 401(k)'s or mutual funds, there is no direct correlation between the amount you contribute and improving results. An IUL gets better as you add more. In fact, the growth maximizes when you need it most during your later years."

"Interesting. So, we should consider finding ways to increase the amount we pay in because we'll get better results that way?" Susan asks.

"Exactly," Michael adds. "Plus, don't forget that you can access that money without having to pay taxes on it under the current IRS tax codes—and as long as you structure and fund the policy correctly. That's why working with an individual agent who understands how the IUL works is so important. If you don't do it

150 Brett Kitchen & Troy Ragan

right, you could lose major tax benefits or miss out on maximizing your cash value growth. This is too important to trust to someone who hasn't had the proper training."

As we step away from the table, it is clear that Jason and Susan are off to a good start on their journey to becoming wealthy outside Wall Street. But, as we leave them to the beginning of their new financial life, we have some shocking revelations to show you.

In the next chapter, we'll show you what might just be the most exciting part of this whole process.

Part of the reason why Jason and Susan can potentially have such a great cash flow in retirement is that the premium payments are used to pay the cost of insurance, and anything above those costs is allocated to an indexed account that receives interest credits based on the performance of the underlying index with an IUL. This allows them to benefit when the market goes up… but never risk their money to loss when it comes down! That's exactly what you'll see in the next chapter.

How to Find Money to Fund an IUL

1. **I'll have that back, thank you.**

    How much is your tax refund each year? Think about changing your deductions to keep more of your income instead of letting the IRS use it for a full year before giving it back to you.

2.   **Redirect your cash flow.**

Often you can redirect money currently going into market investments into an IUL.

3.   **Make your money go to work for you.**

Often funding a policy with excess money you've got in the bank makes sense as an alternate solution for having your money work for you.

4.   **Protect Against Volatility**

This may be a no-brainer if you have money in stocks or mutual funds. Consider moving some money out of the market if you are tired of market volatility.

5.   **Stop the expenses.**

When they add it all up, people are often shocked at how much extra they pay in insurance, utilities, and other everyday expenses. However, making some minor lifestyle changes or just doing a little research on reducing current expenses can help you build your cash value and get on the path of the wealthy.

6.   **In force insurance policies.**

Many people have existing life insurance policies that are not structured as effectively as possible. You may be able to do a 1035 exchange that keeps the cash value and the tax benefits you currently have while improving your results.

7.   **Chopping away at debt.**

Instead of slowly chipping away at debt, consider funding an IUL and then taking a chunk of money and paying off a credit card balance. This could save you a substantial amount on interest costs.

8.   **Splurge on your future.**

Instead of taking the money from your tax return and buying that big screen TV or trip, consider funding an IUL and building on your financial future.

9.   **Extra mortgage payments.**

If you are currently making extra payments to your mortgage principal, consider putting that into an IUL which gives you access to that cash without having to qualify for a loan in order to use it.

Chapter 10

Super Charging the IUL

"The first rule of investing is NEVER LOSE MONEY.
The second rule is NEVER forget rule #1."
—Warren Buffett

I've always wanted to fly. Not in a plane, hot air balloon, or with the help of something man-made. I simply want to look up and take off flying through the air. Unfortunately, I haven't figured out how to make that happen—like the old saying goes: "What goes up must come down."

I learned that the hard way that jumping off the bunk bed as a kid.

As we've discussed, this up and down phenomenon is not limited to physics—it happens quite frequently in the stock market as well. We can have some exhilarating rides up only to suffer financial broken bones when the market comes crashing back down. But it doesn't have to be that way. In this chapter, I'm going to show you how you may just be able to defy market gravity.

One of the most exciting things about an IUL is that you can supercharge the cash value portion of your insurance policy. The policy builds cash value based on premium payments that are above the cost of insurance and other expenses and the performance of the underlying index. One of the benefits of using an IUL is that it's tied to changes in an indexed account, allowing you to enjoy the upside growth of the market while enjoying the protection from negative returns! (You can go up without coming down!)

In other words, the index account in the IUL typically has a floor and a cap. Sometimes you could reach the cap, giving you double-digit returns in years when the market has gains. Likewise, even though you will still have policy fees and expenses, you will not receive negative credit when the market has downturns!

This means when the market goes up, your money can grow (I'll explain more in just a second) *but when the market goes down, you are protected and your money cannot receive a negative credit because of a market downturn, but you will still have policy fees and expenses.* This can be extremely beneficial during times of market turbulence. In years when the market goes up, so do your cash values, and when the market falls, this is where the floor comes in and you receive a zero crediting, and you are protected against that loss. Your money is locked in, so you don't lose! You will sill have to pay the policy fees and expenses.

Now, why is this so important?

It's important because inflation is one of the biggest threats to growing your money and wealth. If inflation is running at 3-5% (or even higher depending on the government's monetary policy), it's important to have your money outpace inflation.

If your money is growing slower than the rate of inflation, you aren't growing your money—you are actually decreasing the value of it over time! The IUL can allow you to outpace inflation by capitalizing on potential growth in the years when the market goes up.

Wait a minute. Didn't I just spend several of the first chapters in this book explaining why the stock market may not be the greatest place to invest your money? Am I changing my tune?

Not at all.

The cash value growth in your indexed universal life policy is *linked to the S&P 500*, but your cash is *not* actually invested *in* the market.

Remember, in Chapter 2, when we showed you the different plunges the market had taken over the years and how long it took to recover and return to even? Now you don't have to deal with that at all!

Your money is protected from any market loss because it is not directly in the market. However, you benefit from the growth of the S&P 500 up to a limit or cap. Let's say the upside cap is 12% (This can vary from policy to policy). This means even if the market goes up 14% or more, your cash value growth would be limited to just 12%.

Having a cap is actually a good thing because this is what allows the insurance company to protect you against losses in those years when the market goes down.

Let's look at a picture that will illustrate this point. This is a hypothetical example of a typical stock market strategy vs. an index strategy.

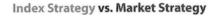

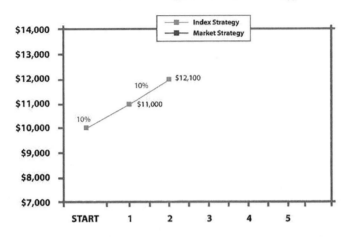

So, let's say you start out with $10,000. And in the first year, the S&P 500 grows by 10%. The first year, there is no difference, and you have $11,000 in either account. In year two, your money grows another 10%. Now you have $12,100 in either account.

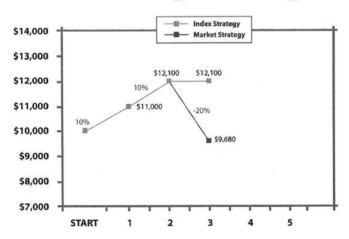

But let's say that in year three, the S&P 500 dropped 20%. Can that happen? Sure, it can. The last few years of the 2000s were worse times than that! Now you would have about $9,600 if you had invested directly in the S&P 500. However, in the indexed strategy, your principal and interest are protected against market loss. So, now instead of $9,600, you hold at $12,100.

Index Strategy vs. Market Strategy

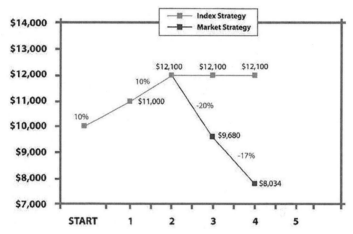

In year four, the market drops another 17%. Now, instead of having $9,600, you have around $8,034. In the indexed strategy, you're still on hold at $12,100.

Now here's the million-dollar question: Do you want $8,034 or $12,100?

That's quite a difference, and it's clear from this example that losing principal can be financially devastating. That's why Warren Buffet said, "it's not so much about the return *on* your money as the return *of* your money." When you lose principal, you've got to get big-time results to bring it back to even.

Now let's look at what happens when the market rebounds. Let's say in year five, the market grows by 15%. In the stock market strategy, the $8,034 would get the full 15% growth, which is about $1,205, so your cash value would climb back up to a little over $9,239. In the indexed strategy, your money would only grow by 12% (remember, we have a cap) to $13,552. But even with the capped growth, you have $13,552 versus $9,239! Again, quite a difference.

Index Strategy vs. Market Strategy

In this example, the downsides of the stock market strategy were:

✓ After five years, you end up with less money than you started with.

✓ It will take a 25% return to get you back to your original $10,000 (and how likely is that to happen in *one* year?)

✓ Even if you did get the 25% you needed, it will only bring you back to $10,000. You just lost *five* years and you are just barely back to even.

Can you see why the indexing strategy is so exciting? Now you can have your money growing when the market goes up, outpace inflation with potential double-digit gains, and never have to worry about losing money when the market goes down.

What kind of peace of mind would that give you—knowing that your money is protected from market volatility?

Now, what would happen if the market went down for 10 years in a row?

Many of the IUL policies can be set up so that there is a fixed interest amount of growth credited to your policy cash values, which guarantees that even if you don't achieve growth in the index, your cash value can continue to grow. (Every policy is a little bit different. That's why it's so important to work with a professional who can show you your options.)

The rest of the IUL benefits still work the same. Meaning, you can Finance Yourself to Wealth™ by accessing your cash value for cars, college, or other major purchases. *Some financial products can even guarantee an income you will never outlive.*

Be sure to ask your insurance professional about this!

Now with all this being said, indexed life insurance doesn't have to be where you put all your money, but for many people, it is an excellent way to position a portion of your portfolio to enjoy the ups of the market without the downside risk.

This is obviously a brief introduction to the indexing strategy to learn more about how this works. Just request a Blueprint at the end of this book, and an insurance professional can help you see it in action and answer your questions.

The Wrap

The indexed strategy makes sense for people who want to avoid market risk but still want the possibility of double-digit gains and all the other benefits that an IUL can give them.

Using this strategy, you could save more money even without changing your current lifestyle by repositioning some of your assets from accounts that are taxed during retirement to an indexed life insurance policy.

The supercharged indexing strategy could allow you to:

- √ Benefit from double-digit gains in up years

- √ Help outpace inflation

- √ Grow your money tax-deferred

- √ Access cash values without incurring tax

- √ Provide cash flow for life

To maximize your growth and give you all the advantages described here, an IUL should be from a life insurance company that meets these requirements:

1. Cash max structure; to maximize cash value and minimize insurance costs
2. 2% guaranteed growth on cash values
3. Flexible loans; so you can switch from variable to fixed loan and back
4. Participating Loans; your money participates in the growth of the index even when you have a loan on the policy.

1. Loyalty bonus on cash values at year 10
2. Decreasing or disappearing charges
3. Very Strong Financially; confirmed by independent rating services
4. Cap that allows *double-digit* growth in good years
5. 100% Participation Rate; so, your cash value grows dollar for dollar when the index grows; (up to the cap).

Chapter 11

More Crash Proof Wealth Strategies

"All truths are easy to understand once they are discovered; the point is to discover them."

—Galileo

Michael smiled as he continued. "The first two Crash Proof Wealth Strategies we discussed were Annuities and Indexed Universal Life (IUL). However, there are three other options I really like for an incredibly effective portfolio. You may not have heard of most of them.

Market-Linked CDs

"The third is a strategy called 'market-linked CDs.' A CD is a Certificate of Deposit. It's a financial product you can put your money into and has two things going for it. It's secure—FDIC insured, just like a bank account—and it gives you a little better rate of return than a savings account, although not much.

"The cons are twofold. A CD does lock your money away for a couple of years, so it's not really very liquid, although you can often get loans by using it as collateral if needed. Plus, the return can be pretty meager when it comes to combating inflation.

But we're talking about something most people have never heard of before. It's an interesting variation to the traditional CD.

"The exciting thing about the *'market-linked'* CD is that you could actually get a higher rate of return than a traditional CD because it's linked to stock market performance.

"What's interesting is that this strategy was developed by big banks and Wall Street firms about 30 years ago specifically for their ultra-rich clients. These clients demanded a better return on their money but still wanted it to be protected. So for years, the ultra-rich have had access to a tool that most average Americans have no idea is even available!"

"I'm not a risk-taker, remember? The stock market makes me a little nervous."

"That's what's neat about this special type of market-linked CD," Michael explained. "You aren't actually risking your money in the market. Your principal is still totally protected and guaranteed, but you get a little more potential growth if the market goes up because your growth is linked to the market."

"Who guarantees it?"

"It's backed by a fully insured FDIC bank— they've just been a bit more creative about how to structure them to allow for a higher rate of return. We'll talk a bit more about the idea of getting the ups of the market with no downside risk. The growth can be much higher than with a typical CD rate."

"Okay, that sounds less frightening. I might even be getting a little bit excited."

Private Real Estate Contracts

"Let's move to a really unique and exciting strategy. It may not be a good fit, but I'll share the basics with you just in case you want to learn more about it. It's something I personally have been using for years, and it's really been my family's hidden secret to creating good returns and financial independence. I learned this from my father, who's been doing it for about 30 years."

"Wow, so this is a secret family recipe, huh?" Jason asked.

"You could say that, although we're now teaching people about it because it's proven to be such a powerful wealth tool for us and works with some of the other strategies we've already talked about. It's called 'private-lending contracts.'

"Private lending is actually a simple concept, but it's mysterious because it's not easy to do. Basically, it involves an individual who has money to lend and a borrower who needs cash. Some of the major benefits of private lending contracts are:

1. Good rates of return: Everyone's results are different; however, those who are really good at this have at times achieved potential annual returns of 12-20% when done properly. There are risks, and this is not for everyone.

2. Managed risk and relative safety: As I mentioned, there is risk; however, while there is definitely risk involved, when you follow the process we share, you reduce your risk and have real property to back it up. What safety net do you have when paper stocks plummet?

3. Control of your money: You call the shots on where your money is invested—you don't depend on someone else to grow your money.

4. Low time commitment: Doing a deal can take as few as 6 hours, including paperwork and traveling to see the property. (There are circumstances when more time is required.)

5. Passive income: Your money is working for you whether you're in the Caribbean or taking a nap on Sunday afternoon! You don't trade hours for dollars anymore.

6. You can do it at any age: With qualified plans, there are all kinds of rules and red tape based on your age. Running a business can become more difficult the older you get. However, you can do private lending at any age because all you have to do is get in the car and go for a drive. My grandfather still does it, and he's in his 80s."

"Wow, that sounds pretty good," Jason said. "Yeah, I hear that a lot. Let me explain how it works so you can understand how you can get these benefits.

"A private-lending contract (PLC) is simply a private loan from one person to another. A traditional bank is not involved. This type of arrangement can offer investors the potential for great returns and low risk when structured properly. The safety comes from securing the loan with collateral, typically a private residential home or commercial building.

Private-lending contracts have a higher interest rate than a bank because of supply and demand. Most people think higher interest rates equate to higher risk. That's typically true. However, the key to making this as secure as possible is to always lend on actual property and always be in first position on the loan."

"Why would anyone borrow money from a private money lender?" Susan asked.

"Good question. It's very simple. Banks have a certain appetite for risk. After 2008, they became even more conservative. Banks won't lend on properties like vacant land or short-term remodeling projects. When an investor sees a good deal, he needs to act fast. In many cases, the banks would never loan on these projects in the first place. Even if you *could* secure traditional financing, acquiring a loan from a bank usually takes a long time and a lot of red tape. In real estate, if you want to get a good deal, you need to act fast, and cash is king.

"This leaves a gaping hole for people who need money and can't acquire financing from a bank. This is where it becomes a win-win for private lenders and borrowers. Our clients don't lose out on a property that will be a good deal for them, and we earn a good interest rate.

"There's more risk to doing this than some of the other strategies, so you need to be very careful with the properties and the borrowers you work with.

"This is not 'no money down' real estate investing. Nor is it buying rental properties. Those may be good strategies, but that's not what we're talking about. This isn't a 'get-rich-quick' opportunity. However, you can grow your wealth when you have a properly structured and funded strategy that could provide you with the potential of your money multiplying faster.

"Combining the strategies of private-lending Contracts with Financing Yourself To Wealth, which I'll show you in a minute, can amplify and multiply your wealth. Combining these strategies is what we call Double Arbitrage.

"Wow, look at the time. I've talked for too long and haven't even covered everything.

"We're always researching and bringing our Wealth Beyond Wall Street family new alternatives when we find them, so this list is by no means static. There is one more strategy we believe in that can give you good returns with more control of your money—I'll cover it quickly."

"We've spoken about the 4th step in the Crash Proof Wealth Framework being Multiply Your Wealth.

"This is not your 'typical' investing strategy, but I'm here because you want to learn how to create financial independence, right?"

"Right," Susan said.

"This last strategy is probably the single most proven and universally used method to create true wealth. In fact, there isn't a millionaire or billionaire I know of who hasn't used this to some degree.

"It's probably not what you're thinking because it's not your typical financial product or investing tool, but I don't want to hold anything back—this is something we're very serious about," Michael said.

"Of course, go ahead. I'd love to know," Jason said.

"Great. The 'strategy' millionaires and billionaires have used to create more wealth than any other single thing is ... business.

"A business can be a great force for good in our world. It raises people out of poverty. It allows us to fulfill our potential, to create and innovate and improve the standard of living of ourselves and those around us. It creates jobs, and it supports and encourages people to achieve great things.

"Just look at how the standard of living in the entire world has skyrocketed in the past 200 years since America was created and free-market capitalism was allowed to work its magic in America and spread across the world. In fact, none of us would enjoy the many luxuries we have without entrepreneurs, innovators, and business owners willing to go out on a limb and risk their capital, their time, their careers, and their innovations to make the world a better place.

"So, something I would consider if you want to accelerate your wealth and have your net worth grow in multiples instead of just growing by percentage points each year is to have your own small (or large) business.

"At first, this sounds daunting to many people, but don't let your initial doubts kill this as an option before you get started. Because starting a business with low risk has never been easier! Approach it with an open mind, you can get started with a skill you already have, or you can sell a product you have access to that you can resell online. Amazon and eBay can do a large majority of the work for you. Increasing your income by $500 to $5000 per month can mean a world of difference for the average person, but when your business really gets going, the income can be truly life-changing.

"It's impossible to build a home—or a mansion, for that matter—without raw materials. Your wealth is the same way. If you don't have enough extra money so that you can put some into savings, your own business can be an answer.

"The purpose of bringing this up today is not to derail our conversation about creating a better way to save money. Rather, it's to give you some food for thought on a time-tested method we have used, and many many others have used, to achieve financial independence.

"Now, one more important thing. Many of these strategies like annuities, private-lending contracts, and even buying a franchise or starting a business can be done using the money you have in qualified plans right now!

"If you have money tied up in a 401(k) or IRA, there are options to access it in a self-directed IRA or other IRAs. That way, you can be in control of where that money is invested.

Just make sure you check with your human resources person regarding accessibility and your tax advisor before doing anything."

The 5 Crash Proof Wealth Strategies

1. Annuities
2. IUL
3. Market Linked CDs
4. Private Real Estate Contracts
5. Entrepreneurship

Like we mentioned, in our experience, the most popular strategy to defeat the enemies of wealth has been in the IUL.

In the next chapter, we'll show you exactly how cash value life insurance impacted the lives of men and women just like yourself. And you'll also recognize some of the biggest names in business that used their cash value life insurance to build their wealth.

Turn the page to see if you recognize a few of these people who, like many of our own policyholders, used the living benefits of life insurance to grow their wealth.

Section 4

EXAMPLES IN ACTION

People seldom improve when they have no other model but themselves to copy after.

—Oliver Goldsmith

Chapter 12

DISNEY, JCPENNEY, MCDONALD'S AND YOU; MAKING IT WORK

"Though no one can go back and make a brand-new start, anyone can start from now and make a brand-new ending."

—CARL BARD

Holly is a 42-year-old New Yorker and a single mother of two.

She has a steady job working in an HR department, making about $33,000 per year, and is having a hard time making ends meet.

Her two kids are in the "expensive" stage of life—middle school and high school—when it seems like every time you turn around, there's another expense to pay for.

She's running ragged, taking care of two kids, working full-time, paying the bills, and keeping the house in order.

It's almost too much for any one person to handle.

Add to it the fact that she's in a seemingly insurmountable amount of debt, and Holly doesn't feel like she's ever going to get out of the hole she's in.

She sees no light at the end of the tunnel—no way out! But it gets worse.

She was actually in more debt than even she realized. After totaling up all the credit cards, lines of credit with stores, and student loans, her debt total, not including her car or home, was over $59,000.

She knew it was bad, but this was a real eye-opener. That was two years' worth of her salary, and $59,000 didn't even count her car or home debt.

She was contributing $100 per month to a company retirement plan, but she knew that wouldn't give her the financial independence she wanted.

The rest of her paycheck each month was going to pay bills or pay down credit card and student loan debt.

Not surprisingly, when we asked her what three financial goals she had, her reply was a lot like you might guess.

First, she'd like to have a little money set aside to take a break and breathe for a weekend or so.

Next, she wants to get out of debt and have some emergency savings put away just in case something comes up with her or her children.

And lastly, she wants to be able to save money for her kid's college funds, and her own retirement.

With only $33,000 of income, $59,000 in consumer debt and college loans, two kids and a mortgage—doesn't this seem like a hopeless case?

Left to her own devices, she really was. She didn't know what to do, and she didn't feel there was any way out of her current situation.

That's where we came in. After reviewing her debts, expenses, and current retirement contributions, we helped Holly put together an IUL, which included a spending and debt analysis. Through that process, we helped Holly find and put away over $500 per month that she was currently wasting!

Over $500 per month on just a $33,000 per year salary!

With our specialized help, she discovered money in multiple areas that she was currently wasting.

Plus, she was able to redirect her current retirement contributions that were currently at risk in the market into an indexed universal life insurance policy to create a nest egg she can count on. She is literally started down the path to becoming wealthy without risking her money!

This might seem hard to believe, but the exciting part is that based on the insurance company projections, by the time she turns 65, she could potentially take out $68,000 per year, every year until age 100! Plus, as long as she does it properly, that money can be accessed without incurring tax!

Imagine her relief when we gave her the IUL blueprint that showed her how, using just her current income, she could create a simple strategy to follow.

This process helped her get out of debt, get her spending under control, and ultimately gave her hope because she now has a blueprint for financial independence.

By steadily putting away money each month, she could have the security of knowing that after age 65, she could have as much as $68,000 per year on just a $33,000 income! Plus, when she does pass on, she'll have a death benefit payable to her two children because of her life insurance policy!

JC Penney

In 1898, James Cash Penney was working in a Golden Rule Store, which was one shop in a small chain of dry goods stores. He turned out to be such an enterprising worker that the pair of owners took him under their wing, offering him a one-third partnership in a new store they were opening. James managed to scrape together $2,000—a pretty significant sum in those days—and opened the new store in Kemmerer, Wyoming.

During the next five years, James helped open two more stores and was doing very well. James focused his efforts on the stores, even investing the extra money he made by working as a lumberjack into them. By 1912 he was running 34 stores throughout the Rocky Mountain region.

The next year, James moved his company headquarters to Salt Lake City, Utah and incorporated under a name you'll easily recognize: The J.C. Penney Company. The JCPenney chain exploded, and by 1929 there were 1,400 stores throughout the nation.

Then things got interesting. The stock market crashed, and the nation was plunged into the depths of the Great Depression.

The depression devastated his stores and his wealth. He was in financial ruin.

Luckily James had not risked all of his money in the market. He had built a cash value insurance foundation. To rebound from the difficult times, he took out a loan from his cash value life insurance policies. He used the cash to meet day-to-day and payroll expenses for his chain of stores. Not only did he keep his head above water, but he also rebounded. Today, the stores take in revenues nationwide of $18.5 billion a year.

As it turns out, that simple cash loan had a greater impact than even James could have realized. Ever heard of Walmart? On a 1940 visit to a JCPenney store in Des Moines, Iowa, James patiently trained a young employee, Sam Walton, showing him how to gift-wrap packages using the least amount of ribbon needed to do the job—and later another retail giant was born.

Doctor Jeff

Jeff thought he was doing pretty well.

He was in his late forties, making a great income as a doctor, and putting $1,000 into his 401(k) every month.

On top of that, Jeff had over $110,000 already socked away. Of course, he wasn't really thrilled that he'd recently lost a big chunk of it in the market crash of 2008, yet despite this setback, *he thought he was still on track for a great lifestyle.*

He wanted financial independence at age 60, and he figured if he could have $70,000-$80,000 per year to live for the rest of his life, he could hang it up whenever he wanted to after 60. However, he was also afraid inflation was going to continue to eat away at his savings.

Jeff wanted to make sure that he could provide his own retirement cash flow. He didn't want to count on social security because, according to the Congressional Budget Office, in 2011, the Social Security Administration was already running a 45 Billion-dollar deficit. And at the end of the day, he wanted to be in control of his finances and retirement, not risk it to someone else.

You could say Jeff thought he had it all under control. In his mind, he was doing everything right; until he saw the truth.

You see, most people have no idea how long their money will actually last after they stop working.

Jeff crunched some quick numbers. He already had $110,000 saved, plus he was adding $1,000 per month to his 401(k). The result was shocking. He discovered that if he continued on his current path, he would only have about $30,000 per year during retirement. And this was BEFORE taxes! Assuming he's in a 20% tax bracket, that's more like $23,400 per year or $2,000 per month!

Right now, Jeff is living off $10,000 per month, so living off just $2,000 per month was like a cold bucket of water right in the face.

But that's not all.

There are other problems with Jeff's current plan.

The money in his current retirement plan is fully taxable, as we showed above; the $30,000 gets taxed when he pulls it out to use it. Plus, if he dies before he retires, his income stops, and he won't have the money built up to provide for his wife or family—there are no guarantees or death benefit. The money is at risk in the market, and the money is tied up in a qualified government plan.

But it gets worse.

This is what really shocked him: For his 80th birthday present, he would be looking at an empty retirement account! That's right, his $2,000 per month would be gone by the time he's 80.

Remember, Jeff wants to retire at age 60. Using the Lifestyle Income Estimator on our website, we showed him that his $2,000 per month could actually run out in less than 20 years!

According to US News and World Report, once a man reaches 65-years-old, life expectancy is 83 years old, and one in every four will live past age 90.[32]

He wondered what type of lifestyle he would have with just $2,000 per month, living with the fear that the money would run out all too soon.

So, we looked at some other options for him.

By using an IUL and working with a life insurance professional—one that specializes in helping people build cash flow that they won't outlive—we came up with a solution that excited and delighted him.

Jeff wanted to see what his retirement would look like if he redirected the $1,000 a month into an indexed cash value insurance policy.

He was comfortable using one of our IUL Insurance Companies because this particular one has been around for over 100 years and has hundreds of billions of dollars in assets around the globe.

After implementing the indexing strategies, Jeff was amazed and excited at his new financial independence blueprint.

Remember, in his current situation, he was looking at running out of money after 15 to 20 years. Plus, this income was fully taxable, didn't have any guarantees, and it was at risk in the market.

With the Indexed policy, his new strategy could give him approximately $69,000 per year—for the rest of his life! And as long as he follows the IRS code properly, he could access that cash flow without a taxable event (according to current IRS tax code).

But that's not all.

In his new IUL, he has no market risk, and if he dies too soon, his family will be protected with the life insurance death benefit. Plus, he has access to the cash value in his insurance policy to Finance Himself to Wealth™ throughout his life!

Like we mentioned before, Jeff was excited about $70,000 per year compared to $24,000…and delighted when he saw this new prospect. Wouldn't you be?

What if you are already in your late fifties or even sixties and don't have a situation like Jeff has. Is it too late?

Thankfully it's not. There are still many options for people of any age, but it's important to start now and not let another day go by without implementing the strategies you have learned here.

Walt Disney

The second household name you'll no doubt recognize involves a man who fought all odds to follow his dream: Walt Disney.[33] Walt and his brother, Roy, were in the animation business. Their story is almost too hard to believe. One of their most popular characters was stolen by another studio. Their best animator jumped ship.

Their studio was chronically understaffed and almost always in debt. In fact, Walt Disney struggled financially for years on the brink of bankruptcy—actually going bankrupt at the age of 21.

Fast-forward to the early 1950s. The only amusement parks in the entire country were horrifically dilapidated places peppered with rusting, creaky rides and known only for their filthy restrooms and the drunks that always hung around. Walt dreamed instead of an immaculately clean amusement park filled with imaginative rides—a place where families weren't afraid to eat the food. World War II had just ended, and the nation was licking its wounds. Walt dreamed of creating an amusement park with an idealized Main Street, U.S.A., where families could identify with something wholesome and good. But that's not all: he dreamed of charging admission to his park and actually making a profit.

Everyone to whom he presented his idea thought he was crazy—and told him so. After all, *no one* charged admission to an amusement park. That just wasn't done. And amusement parks simply couldn't be family-friendly; everyone knew you'd have to sell alcohol if you had a prayer of staying afloat. Even his brother Roy—also his business partner and financial manager—told him it couldn't be done. He urged Walt to forget it. After all, they were in the animation business, not the amusement park business.

Determined to achieve his dream, Walt had no choice but to move ahead on his own. Turned down by traditional financing, he emptied his savings account, sold his vacation home in Palm Springs, and recruited the help of a few employees who shared his vision. Then, he used a loan from his cash value insurance policies to help finance the park. (Roy later admitted he had no idea where Walt's money was coming from but decided not to ask.)

What happened to Walt's dream? Disneyland opened on September 8, 1955, with 18 attractions. It welcomed half a million visitors in the first month it was open. By the end of its first year, it had hosted more than 3.5 million guests. Less than three years later, it welcomed its ten millionth visitor—a number that exceeded well-known national landmarks like Yellowstone and the Grand Canyon. Today, its California Park alone— with more than 60 attractions—has been visited by more than 600 million guests from throughout the world. A dozen of the original attractions from 1955 are still operating in the park today, a testament to Walt Disney's dream of a high-quality, enduring adventure for families.

Stephen G.

Stephen distinctly remembers the day he first knew that nothing could stop him. He had landed a great-paying sales job, and he was also less than a year away from graduating with a degree in business. He was finally on his way up.

It had been a busy year for Stephen. In fewer than 12 months, he had sold his old home—for a tidy profit—and finished building his family's new home. Just as they were unpacking the boxes, his wife announced that they were expecting a baby. They were delighted! Stephen knew life would change and that his cost of living would go up with another mouth to feed, but the idea of his growing family only motivated him to work all the harder.

Life seemed to be moving in the right direction for Stephen.

He'd been with the company for almost a year when the recession of 2008 caused the economy to plummet. The medical specialty that Stephen served was hit particularly hard. Things started to get tough. His income was going down, but his costs weren't.

With his wife at home, caring for their new baby, and with only one income to support the family, money became tight for the first time in their marriage.

Stephen went from comfort and a sense of security to just the opposite. In just 12 months, he went from having $15,000 in the bank to having $15,000 in credit card debt. He went from the joy of building a new home to the fear of losing that home. He went from a feeling of being unstoppable to a gripping sensation of worry. He despaired of ever being able to climb out of debt and replace his savings.

Stephen now had an empty bank account, a whopping credit card debt, two ailing cars, and a home on the verge of being foreclosed. He faced the embarrassment of losing his house, disappointing his family, and starting over. The last straw was his final few weeks at his job—his last three paychecks bounced because the company didn't have the funds to pay him.

Sound hopeless?

It could have been. But something changed for Stephen—and it's the same kind of thing that can change for you. He went back to the drawing board.

Stephen's biggest paradigm shift was realizing the difference between saving and investing. *Saving* is putting your money where there is little risk of losing it. *Investing* is putting your money where you might lose it all.

Stephen also wanted to grow his money while protecting it from taxes. He finally found the solution he was looking for: an IUL. He took what little money he received from his tax refund and started a policy. Despite the terrible economic situation, it changed his entire outlook.

In his own words: "I could create a crystal-clear picture of what my financial future would look like. I could have money in case of emergency or for capital in case a good investment opportunity came up. I could use my cash value to pay for vacations, get out of debt, and send my kids to college, or pay for my retirement.

An IUL gave me a sense of security and gratification, knowing that my money would grow and be available for my use and that my family would be protected and taken care of in case something should happen to me. I have an idea of what my future will look like, I know how much money I will have at certain milestones in my life, and I have a strong financial foundation on which to continue building."

Doris Christopher

Doris Christopher may not be a name you recognize, but the company she founded is. Doris was a successful home economist and educator—but she had a dream. All those hours working with homemakers had convinced her that women needed quality timesaving tools designed to make cooking quick and easy. Women didn't want to spend hours and hours in the kitchen grinding out meals—they wanted to create great meals quickly due to their increasingly busy schedules.

Doris not only had a dream; she had a plan.

Doris's plan involved an army of consultants who would do in-home cooking demonstrations using her professional-quality tools and equipment. Tupperware had done it, and with outstanding success—a homemaker schedules a party, invites her friends and the rest fell into place.

With the support of her husband, Jay, and that of her two young daughters, Doris came up with a detailed business plan and got ready to put it into action. The only thing standing between her and her dream was money.

Her solution was simple. In 1980, Doris borrowed $3,000 from her life insurance policy, and The Pampered Chef was born in the basement of her suburban Chicago home.

In the ensuing decades, the business moved to a series of progressively larger facilities. By 2002, the company had blossomed into a $700 million enterprise acquired by Warren Buffett's Berkshire Hathaway Corporation. Today, The Pampered Chef® has grown into an international corporation serving 12 million customers annually—and it all started with the loan from her life insurance policy.[34]

Angie

To protect her privacy, we won't tell you Angie's last name — but life insurance agent, Rocky, is happy to tell a convincing story about another aspect of the IUL: the legacy we leave to our family when we pass on.

Angie was married to Michael — a 41-year-old anesthesiologist. They were referred to Rocky by another physician, and Rocky met Angie and Michael at their home to discuss their needs. They had a young family—three children under the age of seven. Together they determined they needed $2 million in life insurance coverage.

After a second meeting, during which Michael filled out all of the applications, Rocky also signed him up for $10,000 a month in disability insurance.

Everything went well for the next 18 months. Suddenly, Michael started getting sick. His weight plummeted. He became so weak that it was a struggle to work. A battery of tests revealed no cause for his medical problems, and he became desperate. Almost out of options, he finally talked to a colleague who suggested a latex allergy as the possible culprit. Michael was tested, and sure enough, he was allergic to latex. His allergic reaction was behind the host of symptoms that had plagued him.

With a confirmed latex allergy, Michael had to stop working in the hospital. His disability insurance kicked in, providing an income of $10,000 a month. Yearning to still practice medicine, Michael used some of his disability income and part of his cash value life policy to start a pain clinic—a clinic with a strict ban on latex of any kind.

Things went very well for two years. Then, one night Angie went out to dinner with friends. Michael, who wasn't feeling well, stayed home. That night, Angie found him dead on the bathroom floor. The autopsy results revealed that Michael had contracted bacterial meningitis—and because of the impact that his latex allergy had on his immune system, he didn't have the ability to fight the infection. It killed powerfully and suddenly.

Shortly after that, Rocky delivered a $2 million check to Angie—the amount of the death benefit on the cash value life policy she and Michael had purchased just a few years earlier. Nothing could bring Michael back, but Rocky felt a great sense of satisfaction in helping provide a strong financial future for Angie and her children as a result of their life insurance policy.

Ray Kroc

Ray Kroc came from humble beginnings. Born in Chicago in 1902, at the age of 15, he lied about his age and landed himself a job as an ambulance driver for the Red Cross. Later he actually trained to become an ambulance driver during World War I (where he struck up a friendship with Walt Disney, who was in the same training). Peace treaties were signed before he saw any combat action, so he returned home and tried his hand at a number of jobs—paper-cup salesman, pianist, jazz musician, band member, and radio disk jockey. In a move that would later prove fortuitous, Ray worked at a restaurant in exchange for room and board to learn the restaurant business.

In 1954, at the age of 52, as a milkshake machine salesman, Ray took notice of a hamburger stand in San Bernardino,

California. While most restaurants bought one or two Prince Castle Multi-mixers, which could each mix five shakes at once, the San

Bernardino restaurant had bought eight. Curiosity got the better of Ray Kroc. He wanted to see what kind of restaurant needed to churn forty milkshakes at a time. And so, he set out for California.

What Kroc saw when he got to that restaurant—a hamburger stand owned by Maurice and Richard McDonald—would not only change his life forever but would change the scene of the fast-food industry throughout the world.

Kroc saw the two legendary golden arches and saw lines of people queued up for the restaurant's simple fare of burgers, fries, and milkshakes.

Ray Kroc wanted to slow down as a traveling salesman. His health was declining. He was suffering from diabetes and arthritis, and he had bigger fish to fry. Ray managed to convince the brothers to sell the McDonald's name and trade secrets to him and worked a deal to pay for it with a percentage of the receipts.

McDonald's was on its way to becoming a household name. In 1955, Ray opened his first McDonald's drive-in restaurant in Des Plaines, Illinois.

While things inside the restaurants ran smoothly, Ray faced massive challenges with cash flow, franchises, competition, and the economy in general. He was determined to be successful and spent year after year, working day and night, to build his company.

In order to build the largest fast-food chain in the world and overcome constant cash-flow problems, Ray took out loans on two cash value life insurance policies to get his infant company off the ground. He used some of the money to create an enduring advertising campaign centered on the company's mascot, Ronald McDonald.

Ray Kroc passed away from old age in January 1984 at the age of 81, just 10 months before McDonald's sold its fifty-billionth hamburger. At the time of his death, there were some 7,500 McDonald's restaurants worldwide. Today, with more than 25,000 restaurants worldwide, McDonald's is the world's largest foodservice retailer, with operations in more than 65 countries.

The Wrap

What did you learn from James Cash Penney, Doctor Jeff, Walt Disney, Stephen G., Doris Christopher, Angie, and Ray Kroc?

There are important lessons in every one of these examples. You can work as hard as humanly possible. You can make all the right plans. But when the financial storms come, they can be devastating if you have a weak financial foundation. But, if you have the right financial foundation in place, you can withstand them. By having the foundation of a cash value insurance policy in place, you can keep your money safely growing outside of the market. You can have the peace of mind you are looking for.

And here's the really great news. It's not hard or complicated. You don't have to know it all.

Remember what you learned from Aristotle in the opening pages of this book: "Money is a guarantee that we may have what we want in the future."

You can't go back in time and change your beginning, but you can start today and make a brand new ending.

Chapter 13

Bonus Chapter: For Business Owners Only

"The entrepreneur is our visionary, the creator in each of us. We're born with that quality, and it defines our lives as we respond to what we see, hear, feel, and experience."

— MICHAEL GERBER

If there's a portion of the country that is underserved and underappreciated, it might just be the small business owner.

I know firsthand because I have been one for the better part of a decade, and my family has a long genealogy of small business owners.

It goes all the way back to my great-great-grandfather, who was a watchmaker on Jersey Isle in England.

From there, we have my great-grandfather who owned a painting construction business. My grandfather ran multiple businesses and my father built the largest boat trailer manufacturing company in the mountain west area.

Being a business owner is tough.

I know what it's like to have the stress of overhead, payroll, advertising to get new clients, economic forces outside of our control, late hours, missed soccer games, and the huge amount of risk we take on. We do it all because we want to provide financial security for our families and live the American Dream of financial success.

Most of us don't get benefit packages that someone else is paying for. Usually, no one is contributing to *our* retirement plan. We don't punch a time clock or have the luxury of having someone else cut us a check every two weeks.

It's common knowledge that the small business owner is the engine of the American economy. Yet too often, we work ourselves to death and continually pour any extra money back into the business, often neglecting our own savings as we try to build our companies.

If you are anything like me, we approach our business with a case of never-ending faith that next week, month, or year we'll make the money we want. And soon months and years have passed, and we've invested everything back into the business and haven't stashed anything away for ourselves.

Joining the ranks of the wealthy beyond Wall Street could change that right now.

Not only can an IUL create an "automatic wealth-building machine" where you put money away each month without thinking about it, but you can still access that money for use *in* your business.

Let's talk about three simple ways you can be using an IUL to save money, prepare for the future and help your business grow.

Finance Yourself to Wealth™

If you buy equipment, vehicles, or own real estate for your business or investments, this is for you.

Funding an IUL can be done in a couple of different ways.

You can start by simply putting in a set amount of money each month, then borrowing against that cash value to buy whatever you need for your business.

You can also start a policy by dumping in a one-time payment like $20,000, $50,000, or even $100,000 and using that as your own source of funding. It's kind of like your own private source of financing, except no qualifying is necessary to use the cash!

Use your IUL to buy business equipment, vehicles, or real estate by using the money in your policy, and it still grows as if you've never touched it.

Instead of going out and buying a truck for your company the old way, use your policy to finance your purchase, then recoup the cost of the truck by paying your insurance loan back.

You can even get more advanced by using these policies as a separate entity that acts as a leasing company that purchases vehicles, real estate, and other equipment.

If the Worst Should Happen

Have you ever heard of a business getting destroyed because a partner dies and the spouse comes in to take over the interest with no experience whatsoever?

I really do like my business partner's wife, but she and I running a business together would not be a pretty picture.

It happens more often than you might think. In fact, take a look at these sobering statistics.

These figures show the likelihood, out of 100, that one of two business partners in good health will die before they're 65:

Age of Business Owner	Chances
40/40	35%
45/45	33%
50/50	29.9%
55/55	24.7%

If there are three partners, the percentages are much higher.[35]

So what does that mean for you and your business? If you have a partner, or two, you can use an IUL insurance policy to fund a buy-sell agreement. This would provide you with cash to buy out that partner's ownership of the business if they should die. The company can continue to thrive without the disruption of a new partner, and the spouse of the partner will be compensated fairly.

But it gets even better than that.

Let's go for the best-case scenario. Assume you and your partner both live long, healthy lives.

You get to enjoy all the living benefits of the IUL throughout your lives the same way we already have described previously. Use it for vehicle financing, major purchases, funding growth, or buying real estate.

This is ultimately where you probably want to be.

We've hopefully already established in black and white why a solid financial foundation is the key to a great lifestyle— but why not use this powerful tool to grow your business, save you money on interest throughout your life, and then enjoy a passive stream of cash flow that comes from your policy as you travel to exotic destinations with your spouse, golfing the days away, and enjoying the fruits that you worked so hard for.

> *"The single biggest benefit in the tax code is the tax exemption for life insurance."*
>
> —ED SLOTT,
> THE RETIREMENT SAVINGS TIME BOMB

If all the living benefits weren't enough to convince you that an IUL should be a part of your financial plan, this might.

Willie Sutton and the Tax Man always follow the money.

Estate taxes can be over 50% of your estate, and that's not just liquid funds. It could include residential and commercial real estate, investments, and all the assets you may have. Often people underestimate their estates, yet they can add up to $800,000 to $1,000,000 fairly quickly.

Imagine the problem your family could have when they get a tax bill saying they owe $500,000, and much of that is tied up in real estate.

This is especially problematic if the real estate market is down, and people have to "fire sell" at below market value just to satisfy the demands of the tax man.

Here's where the IUL really shines.

Under the current IRS tax code, life insurance death benefits are paid out income tax-free. This means they come to the estate or your family (depending on how the policies are set up) in a lump sum. You can use that money to pay the estate taxes while protecting your other hard-earned assets.

Life insurance payouts *are* usually subject to estate taxes, so keep that in mind when you calculate how much insurance you'll need to cover the entire tax bill...and as always, consult with a proper estate tax planning professional.

This is where a professional life insurance agent could really help you. Not only can they help you with an IUL but also with asset protection, estate tax planning, and other issues to help build a strategy for protecting and growing your wealth. Just go to www.crashproofwealth.com.

Endnotes

1 https://www.newretirement.com/retirement/podcast-episode-11-bob-merton-fixing-retirement/

2 https://www.newretirement.com/retirement/podcast-episode-11-bob-merton-fixing-retirement/

3 https://www.morningstar.com/articles/980620/wade-pfau-the-4-rule-is-no-longer-safe

4 https://retirementresearcher.com/long-can-retirees-expect-live-hit-65/

5 https://www.annuity.org/2019/07/03/deferred-annuities-improve-retirement-outcomes/

6. FDIC.gov; Foreclosure statistics

7. AFL-CIO analysis of 292 companies in the S&P 500 Index. CEO pay data provided by salary.com.

8. Barry James Dyke, *Pirates of Manhattan*

9. Nelson Nash, *Becoming Your Own Banker*

10. Barry James Dyke, *Pirates of Manhattan*

11. http://www.davemanuel.com/inflation-calculator.php

12. http://business.time.com/2013/03/12/if-theres-no-inflation-why-are-prices-up-so-much/

13. http://news.bbc.co.uk/2/hilbusiness/3746044.stm, Monday, 1 November, 2004, news.bbc.co.uk

14. http://www.kiplinger.com/magazine/archives/2008105/hidden-401(k)-fees.html#ixzz13CwvXJKI

15. Damien Hoffman, *Cramer Buy Recommendation CIT Goes Bankrupt*, Wall St. Cheat Sheet, Nov. 1, 2009.

16. Bill Alpert, *Cramer :S Star Outshines His Stock Picks*, Baron :S , Feb. 9, 2009.

17. Ira Rosen, *The 401(k) Fallout*, 60 Minutes

18. FBI History, Famous Cases, Willie Sutton, www.jbi.gov

19. http://wwwjorbes.com/forbes/201010426/investing-obama-tax-hikes-capital-gains-duck-obamatax.htmI

20. Scott Shultz, www.avoidthedeferraltrap.com

21. Becoming Your Own Banker, Nelson Nash

22. William Wolman and Anne Colamosca, *The Great 401(k) Hoax: Why Your Family's Financial Security Is at Risk and What You Can Do About It* (Cambridge, MA: Perseus Publishing, 2002), 12.

23. *The Outer Limits, Some of These Funds Go Way Beyond the*

Ordinary, Forbes, September 18, 2006.

24. Anthony Mirhaydari, *MSN Money.* The following adapted from Barry James Dyke, *The Pirates of Manhattan: Systematically Plundering the American Consumer and How to Protect Against It* (Hampton, NH: 555 Publishing, Inc., 2008), 69-76.

25. http://www.miravast.com/Images/BH_Miravast_LSR_07192013. pdf

26. http://www.livinghistoryfarm.org

27. http://blogs.wsj.com/deals/2010111108/tracking-bank-failures-2010-tops-2009-for-bank-failures/

28. *Pirates of Manhattan*, Barry James Dyke

29. Ed Slott, *The Retirement Savings Time Bomb ... and How to Diffuse It.*

30. In the event of a lapse, outstanding policy loans in excess of unrecovered cost basis will be subject to ordinary income tax. Tax laws are subject to change. Be sure to consult a tax professional beforehand.

31. Based on illustration of 42 year old male, preferred health, using an A Rated Indexed Life Insurance Company illustration using a 5.0% variable loan rate and 7.5% monthly growth cap.

32. http:l/.finance.yahoo.com/focus-retirement/article/110176/predicting-your-life-expectancy?mod=fidelity readytoretire&cat=fidelity_2010_getting_ready_to_retire

33. Adapted from Catherine and Richard Greene, *The Man Behind the Magic: The Story of Walt Disney* (NY: Viking Penguin, 1991).

34. (Currency/Doubleday, 2005) and *Come to the Table: A Celebration of Family Life* (Warner Books, 1999).

35. http://www.raricklaw.com/assets/pdf/client-newsroom/20091

36. Michael Lewis, *Flash Boys*.

37. https://wealthicity.com/interview-with-suze-orman-will-have-you-question-her-advice-and-integrity/

38. https://taxfoundation.org/us-federal-individual-income-tax-rates-history-1913-2013-nominal-and-inflation-adjusted-brackets/

39. Business Insider (http://www.businessinsider.com/2009/2/america-lost-102-trillion-of-wealth-in-2008)

40. Real World Index Annuity Returns." Wharton Financial Institutions Center. (http://summitalliance.net/wp-content/uploads/2010/04/Wharton-Study-Real-World-Index-Annuity-Returns.pdf)